WILDCAT CURRENCY

ЭNOVA

WILDCAT
CURRENCY

HOW THE

VIRTUAL MONEY

REVOLUTION

IS TRANSFORMING

THE ECONOMY

Yale UNIVERSITY PRESS/NEW HAVEN & LONDON

This material is based upon work supported by the National Science Foundation under Grant No. 1049449. Any opinions, findings, and conclusions or recommendations expressed in this material are those of the author(s) and do not necessarily reflect the views of the National Science Foundation.

Yale University Press books may be purchased in quantity for educational, business, or promotional use. For information, please e-mail sales.press@yale.edu (U.S. office) or sales@yaleup.co.uk (U.K. office).

Designed by Mary Valencia.
Set in Bulmer MT Pro type by IDS Infotech, Ltd.
Printed in the United States of America.

Library of Congress Cataloging-in-Publication Data
Castronova, Edward.
Wildcat currency: how the virtual money revolution is transforming the economy /
Edward Castronova.
pages   cm
Includes bibliographical references and index.
ISBN 978-0-300-18613-0 (hardback)
1. Money. 2. Tokens. 3. Exchange. 4. Value. I. Title.
HG231.C344 2014
332.4—dc23   2013041269

A catalogue record for this book is available from the British Library.

This paper meets the requirements of ANSI/NISO Z39.48-1992 (Permanence of Paper).

10 9 8 7 6 5 4 3 2 1

For Doris

CONTENTS

ACKNOWLEDGMENTS

The original impetus for this work came from a meeting organized by the Federal Reserve Banks of Atlanta and Cleveland. I thank Dave Altig, Mike Bryan, Bruce Champ, and Timo Henckel, four outstanding monetary economists, for putting these ideas in my head.

I was fortunate enough to receive financial support from an anonymous donor as well as from the National Science Foundation under the program direction of William Sims Bainbridge, a profound thinker on religion and technology.

I could not have done the grant work without Travis Ross, my research assistant. Actually, scratch that. I did not do the grant work; Travis did. He winnowed down the vast universe of virtual worlds into a manageable subset for exploration; he hired the undergraduates to do the exploring; he wrote the content document they used; he summarized the findings. Travis was a true collaborator and deserves equal billing on this project, even though he did not have a hand in writing the book.

I'd like to thank Michael Chabin for great lunch conversations, and my chairman Walter Gantz for his quiet, compassionate leadership and mentoring.

The anonymous reviewer has my gratitude for catching and correcting some pretty severe conceptual errors.

And now, my editor, Bill Frucht. An editor is a strange bird, happy to do something that drives the rest of us crazy: Constantly remind (and re-remind and re-re-remind) people who should know better to stop writing that one bad thing, that one turn of phrase or sentence structure that deeply offended when first encountered yet reappears again and again. Each time, Bill Frucht dutifully crossed out "loan" when used as a verb, and replaced it with "lend." Whenever Bill saw "The thing about this is that this is a new question," he quietly wrote, "This is a new question," even though he had done so five hundred times already. Did you know that most *Important Points* in a book are actually not capitalized, italicized, or expressed in bold type? I didn't. Bill does. Guess how many of these things he had to quash? The mind boggles. And on top of all this, Bill kept my mind focused on the right issues with pointed, deep questions and comments throughout. Best editor I've had; thank you, Bill.

Special thanks to Annie Lang, my colleague at Indiana University, who read my last book thoroughly and gave extensive comments only to be ignored accidentally in the acknowledgments. Oops. Annie: thank you for your laughter, wisdom, and sharp thinking through the years.

There are no words to express my gratitude to my wife, Nina, and my boys Luca and Malcolm.

I dedicated the book to my grandmother Doris Ball Bird, who was a country school English teacher. She pushed me to further my education, and also made it financially possible.

Finally: thank you, God, for putting me on the Earth and giving me a chance to breathe the air for this short time.

INTRODUCTION

As recently as 2003, the term "virtual currency" had only limited relevance. Casino chips and frequent flyer miles were kinds of virtual currency, as were the play-money "gold pieces" of a handful of online games. Efforts to launch virtual eCash systems had uniformly failed. But the past decade has been a time of massive currency innovation and expansion. The virtual money economy is now larger than the economies of many real countries.[1]

Any discussion of a currency is ultimately about how traders exchange value. The purpose of a payments system is to allow people to trade other things quickly and easily. Payments systems that do this job better have historically pushed out those that do it worse. Coins replaced barter and were replaced by paper, which in turn has yielded to electronic transactions. Virtual currencies are part of the next step, which is too new even to have a name. Let's call it digital value transfer, or DVT. A DVT is an electronic payments system that seamlessly transfers purchasing power among users and currencies.

The difference between DVT and current electronic payments systems is this: With an electronic payments system, various entities (banks, stores, employers) use computers to report to one another the ownership of state-sanctioned currencies like dollars and euros. Paper is unnecessary: you simply indicate in a database how many dollars or euros are owned. Yet each account is still locked into a single metric of value—you own dollars, yen, or whatever. A digital value transfer system is not locked into any one metric. Instead, it maintains a table of exchange rates between any number of ways to denominate value, and uses this table to seamlessly transfer value between entities. My account may be in dollars and yours may be in Delta Frequent Flyer Miles, and it doesn't matter. The payments system knows how to translate one into another. You can pay for the chocolate candy bar I am selling using Delta Miles, Warcraft Gold, or yen. A DVT payments system handles them all.

We can already see how digital currency leads to more fluid value transfer. Consider the Facebook payments system. A Facebook application developer can create any kind of currency for his app. If he makes a game, perhaps the currency is "sillies," and you get sillies by playing the game. But you can also use dollars to buy sillies directly from the developer. Sillies represent a revenue stream for the developer, and Facebook handles the payments. The developer tells Facebook how much he wishes to charge for sillies, and when players buy sillies, they transfer their money to Facebook, which then generates the sillies for their account in the game. When the developer wants to cash out, Facebook gives him dollars according to the stated silly-per-dollar exchange rate, minus a hefty fee (at this writing, 30 percent). Facebook provides this service for many thousands of application developers. It thus operates as a bank that can seamlessly translate value among thousands of currencies. In 2012, that bank processed more than $800 million in transactions where dollars were paid for virtual goods.[2] Right now, Facebook does not allow people to use money from one application to buy things in another. But it could; the walls separating Facebook's currencies are not economic or technological, or even legal. Facebook simply chooses to keep them separate.

Facebook could, if it wished, remove the walls between its currencies and make itself into a huge economy. As the sole monetary regulator for this vast realm, it could issue its own money. In fact, it did for a time; the currency was called "Facebook credit." But then it chose to create a digital value transfer system—a world of currencies instead of just one.

Currencies are blooming everywhere. According to the European Central Bank, there is already more monetary value in customer-loyalty currencies (such as frequent flyer miles) than is held in the physical form of notes and coins.[3] A game called Diablo III allows players to gather virtual gold in the game and then sell it directly to other players for real money. The designers of the Bitcoin virtual currency clearly intended it to operate as a global currency but not as a "real" one. As I am writing, the massive online retailer Amazon has announced the launch of its own virtual currency, the Amazon Coin. Almost every social media system deployed today— and there are thousands and thousands, occupying the attention of billions of people—uses some kind of virtual currency. World of Warcraft's ten million subscribers have massive accounts of Gold Pieces. The twenty million users of the Xbox system can spend their Microsoft Points to rent movies from Netflix. In 2007, the Central Bank of China banned the exchange of renminbi against a game currency called QQ Coins because too many people were using redeemable QQ Coin cards to buy things in the real economy. Even brick-and-mortar companies are getting into the act, morphing their frequent-buyer reward programs into accounts with broad purchasing power. Inventing currencies is a common business practice. The obvious next step is connecting them.

How these connections are made, and who sees them, will clearly influence economic growth and the power of the state in the twenty-first century. While we can only guess at what this influence will be, there are some points of information. Virtual currency is a not a new phenomenon. Prisoners have used cigarettes as money. Your grandmother may have collected S&H Green Stamps, which she pasted into a book and then was able to redeem for a toaster or a sewing machine. For much of the early 1920s, the German mark was play money. Confederate government bonds were real money in 1862 and play money in 1866. The emergence of wildcat currency, with its tremendous flexibility and power, seems likely to spark a broad-ranging discussion of what money is and what it is for.

The trend over the past few centuries has been the other way, toward fewer currencies. Economists and monetary policy authorities have long taught that economies do better with just one form of money. The experts decided long ago that multiple currencies within a jurisdiction, which were once common, are a headache. When there are many currencies, no one knows the worth of even a mildly complex portfolio: each item is expressed in different money with a different value. The costs of exchanging money to obtain purchasing power in a different jurisdiction are a pure loss. Speculation in currencies is natural, because a currency's value ultimately depends on what people expect its value to be in the future. But the chaotic monetary conditions that result encourage financial panic. For these reasons and more, financial policymakers have moved, over the centuries, to reduce the number of currencies in the world and to keep those that remained under tight regulation.

The profusion of new and unregulated currencies thus raises problems. Are we about to reverse the trend toward a single global currency? Are we going back to a preindustrial system, where every king, prince, and duke issued his own money? That old system was prone to booms and busts, along with multiple layers of confusion. That was why it was gradually replaced by the money system we have today, with only a few "hard" currencies whose value is kept fairly stable. Are we returning to a more chaotic state? Or can we rely on digital systems to handle the complex flow of many monies?

There are other worries. How do you regulate a digital value transfer system? Should you? Is it legal to prosecute people who issue their own currencies? How do people make money with a virtual currency? Can we predict how the system will evolve? If we want to be ready for the economic future, what should we be doing now?

Between September 2010 and August 2011, I directed a National Science Foundation–funded research team devoted to surveying the development of emerging economic institutions in the gray area between the virtual and the real.[4] We did case studies of some important products in internet space and sent research assistants on exploratory missions into more than two dozen online media systems. One result stood out: every single one of these places had an internal market with its own currency. Every one of those currencies could be exchanged against the U.S. dollar, either in a reasonably robust market or through direct sales with a reputable company. The global metasystem of digital value transfer is already here, waiting to leap into public view.

Most normal people (meaning those without a degree in economics) think of virtual worlds as "not real" and significantly different from "the real world." Strictly speaking, of course, this has never been quite true, and many scholars have now abandoned the distinction. A phone call is a real conversation even though it is happening via computers over the internet. When five boys team up in an online game to attack a dragon, their teamwork is no less real than the teamwork of five boys on a basketball team. The dragon-hunting environment may be computer-generated, and the behaviors may be computer-mediated, but the boys are still boys. Still, "virtual" versus "real" is a convenient shorthand that I will use throughout this book. An observation like "Activity X is common in the virtual world but not in the real world" is a convenient way to contrast human interaction in computer-generated spaces with human interaction in non-computer-generated spaces. When I say such things, I am not assuming that anything is or is not real. Rather, I am identifying two distinct arenas of human behavior, using the words "virtual" and "real" much as I might use "France" and "America." Readers should note, however, that the continents are colliding. The emergence of wildcat currency is a sign that real and virtual continue to blend.

I have organized the book into two parts, the first about the status of wildcat currency today and the second about its implications. Chapters 1 and 2 provide a brief history of money, as a context within which to think about the innovation of virtual currency.

People have been inventing money for a very long time, and the reasons for doing so have not really changed. What's changed is the technology of managing payments. Today, anybody can be a central bank.

In Chapters 3 and 4, I address two concrete questions that arise immediately. First, is any of this legal? Can people just *invent* money? The answer, at least in the United States, is yes. There are no legal restrictions on "private money." Second, is this stuff really money? A fellow can declare himself a central bank and start issuing certificates with his name and picture, but that does not mean that the certificates are money. Money has a definition, and in Chapter 4 I examine whether wildcat currencies meet that definition. Most do.

In Part II I get into the implications. Chapters 5 and 6 concern the implications of currency chaos for two important aspects of economic health. In Chapter 5 I look at money's role in measuring and communicating value. A currency system that makes it hard to do those things imposes great burdens on the economy, slowing trade and growth. In Chapter 6 I examine the issue of confidence. A currency system that raises doubts about its own stability creates the conditions for panic. Past financial panics have had disastrous consequences well beyond the economy. It is wise therefore to consider whether a vast system of virtual currencies encourages too much doubt.

In Chapter 7 I outline the probable course of the wildcat currency phenomenon. There will probably always be incentives to create new currencies, and economic actors will generally want to use a payment system that best suits their needs. Those needs will vary: different actors will embrace different degrees of legality and will not be equally willing to conform to regulation. Currency innovation is thus likely to persist and move toward a broad digital value transfer system.

Chapter 8 and the Epilogue conclude the book with a discussion of government responses to wildcat currency creation. How do these developments affect economic governance? Can we learn something about statecraft from the way private actors manage their economies? As the boundary between dollars and gold pieces blurs, it smudges many other borders that we hold dear.

These developments suggest at least two concrete policy recommendations:

Lines must be drawn. There is no natural, technical, or economic line between the institutions of a virtual community and those of a real one. There is not even a reason to contrast the terms "real" and "virtual." It's all real. Both economies run on the internet. While convention makes it convenient to use "real" to refer to brick-and-mortar economies and "virtual" to refer to social media economies, the distinction is conceptual, not concrete. Yet it is extremely important to keep in mind the different *goals* economies might have. Game economies and marketing economies have radically different purposes: one exists to entertain, the other to sell. The line that should be drawn between them is based not on any technical difference but on their different contributions. A game is supposed to make us happy; how unhappy would we be to find our game earnings taxed like real earnings! A marketing scheme is supposed to sell things; how unfair it would be not to tax the resulting profits as real earnings! Lines must be drawn according to the institutions' purposes.

Test your policy. Second, the emergence of virtual currency has revealed a new approach to public policy. Virtual currencies were birthed in an industry steeped in testing as a development protocol. No game company releases a new product without testing it first with real people. When virtual currencies came to be noticed, they had already been refined by thousands upon thousands of hours of practical experience in games. Governments should learn from this. As the boundaries between public policy and social media development continue to blur, governments will increasingly be expected to test their proposals in virtual worlds before unleashing them on us.

People's growing tendency to spend time in fantasy environments is beginning to have economic consequences.[5] Ten years ago, 5.7 percent of Americans bought a new car in a given year. Today it's down to 4.9 percent.[6] Car sales dipped heavily in 2008 as a result of that year's financial crisis. But why have they recovered so slowly in the years since then? The population has continued to grow, but as I write this in 2013, car sales are still below their precrash level. And cars are not unique: many other consumer products are showing similar patterns of stagnant recovery.[7] There could be many explanations, but one possibility is a gradual shift into a more internet-centric lifestyle, in which tangibles are less important.

But more is going on than large numbers of people leaving the real world for the fantasy world. The fantasy world is also leaping out into the real world. Virtual currencies are gaining importance not because more people are playing online video games but because people are using them for ordinary economic transactions. We are living through a period in which technology is making fantasies concrete. In some cases, we see people using technologies to go live in dream worlds. In many others, though, technology is transforming the institutions of dream worlds into those of the real world. The real importance of virtual currency is what it tells us about the merging of the game world with the outside.

PART I

THE CURRENCY EXPLOSION

I t has gotten hard to deny that there are a lot of funny currencies out there.

Gamers have been dealing in virtual money for a long time. Anyone who plays a game with an online multiplayer component expects it to have some sort of virtual currency—a gold piece or credit or doubloon by which to measure the acquisition of wealth. This is such an integral part of the experience that most players would be surprised to find a virtual world *without* a currency. Most single-player games go farther: they have fake economies in which players can sell things they have acquired to nonplayer merchants in return for virtual currencies. The difference between single-player and multiplayer is only that the trades in multiplayer games are between two real humans. In that case, the market is a lot less play and a lot more real. As an economist who is a gamer, I have taken note of these currencies over and over. They are as familiar to me as bushes and trees are to a landscaper.

These days, however, you don't have to be a gamer (or an economist!) to notice virtual currencies. Casual observers of business, new media, and the internet are starting to encounter virtual money everywhere. It has long existed at a low level, in marketing schemes like frequent flyer miles and Green Stamps and bonus points. Buy ten cups of coffee, get the eleventh free. Nothing remarkable there. But as the world has gone digital, it has become much easier for anybody to launch and manage a sophisticated points system. Lots of companies are now in this game. Every major credit card has a points system, every major retailer, every social media app. Several years ago, they expected you to keep a special card that made you part of their "club." If, unlike Groucho Marx, you were willing to join any club that would have you as a member, you'd have points in a thousand clubs and a thousand cards in your pocket to keep track of them all. Now the need for cards has vanished—just register with the company, and every time you buy there, your rewards account increases. Salads, books, shoes, beer, or virtual farmland—whenever you make a move in the contemporary economy, you build up points somewhere. They are worthless until they are cashed in.

But "cashed in" does not mean that you literally turn them into dollars, euros, or yen. (What *is* cash in this environment? More on that later.) "Cashed in" means you use them to buy something that has value, like a cup of coffee or a new book. What if you use them to buy more virtual farmland? Did you just trade nothing for nothing? What if you could cash in credit card points to buy a card that lets you subscribe to a new game for a month? Or gold pieces in a game?

Or it could go the other way: you could cash in gold pieces from a game to get points on your credit card, which you could use to buy a bagel. That eventuality is not far away. The point is, you don't have to be a gamer to encounter virtual currencies all the time. They grew up in games, but now they're everywhere.

1

WEIRDLY NORMAL
VIRTUAL ECONOMIES AND
VIRTUAL MONEY

When my students and I began our research project, we thought our goal was to examine the growth of shadow economies on the boundary between the real and the virtual. By "real" we meant offline or brick-and-mortar economies, and by "virtual" we meant the economies of video games and social media systems like Facebook. We were especially interested in gray areas like the Amazon trading platform or the Steam marketplace.

After a lot of time spent looking at different examples of virtual economies, we chose twenty-seven of them as representatives of various sectors of the social media world. We developed a lengthy content analysis questionnaire and hired several assistants to go into each environment and answer as many of the questions as possible. We asked, for example, whether the social media environment had a marketplace and if so, whether it was heavily used. We also asked how real resources like time and money affected the experience of the virtual environment, and whether they contained other aspects of a normal economy such as wages, banks, or production.

These environments, we found, contain tremendous economic, social, and cultural diversity. Yet there was one striking common factor: every world we explored had its own virtual currency. Anyone who launched a social networking project of any kind was introducing his or her own currency. Like the wildcat oilmen of the past century, currency builders were rushing to capitalize on a money-making opportunity that, for now, proceeds with no government oversight whatsoever.

The first thing most people ask me, when I describe my research at cocktail parties, is, "How much money are we talking about?" It is very hard to say. First, are we talking about virtual economies, or the currencies that support them? There are no generally accepted public data on the size and growth of either one. Virtual goods are being generated and traded all over the world, with a rapidity and ease made possible by the simple fact that these are all digital entities. The situation would have thrilled Plato, intellectual father of The Forms: here we have a bewildering cloud of things, all of which are definite, distinctly identifiable things as such, and some of which have clear economic value. Yet none of them has a physical manifestation. The physical traces these things leave—and they're only traces—are electrical signatures on memory chips. Those signatures come and go in response to computer program commands; they are just footprints on the seashore, washed away almost at once. The things themselves are merely notions. How can one begin to describe such a chaotic, fluid phenomenon?

One way might be to take a direct measure of virtual-goods transactions and assign them a dollar value. This is a massive task, not because of too little information but because of too much. Markets in virtual worlds typically spawn tremendous amounts of data, on trading, prices, and transactions. In many virtual economies, the data are streamed to the user's client computer and transferred directly into a common data analysis software package. A statistician has only to enter the virtual world and record the numbers as they come to the screen. But making sense of the information is not easy. The data stream produced by a virtual world is immense but completely disaggregated.[1] It consists of many thousands of time-stamped records of item-for-item trades, such as One Bolt of Linen Cloth for Twelve Gold Pieces. The companies themselves generally do not create economic aggregates for their own analysis and management.[2] While is possible to clean the data and analyze a virtual economy as a "normal" economy, it is an immense task.[3]

A more manageable but indirect way to get a global sense of virtual economies, if not currencies, is to consider virtual item sales: how much real-world money a company makes from its customers' purchases of virtual goods. One recent estimate put the virtual goods market at $15 billion per year.[4] A recent report of the European Central Bank estimates that the amount of real money people paid to acquire game and social media virtual currencies (so-called "real money trade" or RMT) lay between $200 million and $10 billion in the years 2008–2010.[5]

But an estimate based on the virtual goods market fails to count everything in virtual economies that has value. Transactions of virtual goods for real currencies represent only a small part of a virtual economy. They do not count the value of virtual goods traded for virtual currency, or those produced for self-consumption. Such items have economic value even though they are not sold for real money. Hence the statistics generally underrepresent the significance of the economy they are measuring. It is like measuring the scope of the Japanese economy by counting only the value of Japanese goods that are purchased with U.S. dollars, while ignoring goods purchased with yen or consumed by the people who produced them. In a virtual economy, most virtual goods are consumed directly by the producer. Most of the rest are traded to other users using the in-world currency. Sales of virtual goods and currency for dollars are the tip of the iceberg.

The most reasonable assessments that we have indicate that virtual currencies—including game currencies, digital currencies, and customer-loyalty currencies—constitute a substantial and rapidly growing phenomenon. Nonetheless, the European Central Bank concludes that there is not much to worry about—yet.

WHY ARE VIRTUAL CURRENCIES IMPORTANT? FOUR EXAMPLES

So why should we care? Although virtual currencies and virtual economies are not on many people's radar, their explosive growth rate suggests that they will quickly become an extremely important part of the world economy. Almost every social media product we studied, whether game, service, or business, carried with it a virtual currency. To the makers of these worlds, having a currency seemed entirely natural, even necessary, even if the product was not a fantasy or a game. With customer-loyalty programs, it seemed as though everyone who runs a business has decided to make his or her own currency.

Moreover, a currency is only one element of a payments system. It is possible to conceive of a payments system with no fixed currency. Virtual currencies point to a future of seamless digital value transfer. The four examples below show how virtual currencies offer easy solutions to economic, social, and commercial needs. Their emergence and application seem quite natural. They "work." This functionality might explain why we found virtual currencies in every environment we studied.

MAGIC THE GATHERING

The first example actually has nothing to do with the internet. But because it shows how easily a virtual currency can be launched and then used for trades among a large group of people, it provides a good look at the basic mechanisms by which play money becomes real money.

Magic the Gathering is a card game launched in 1993. Until 2002 it had no formal presence on the internet. Yet it spawned an economy and generated trade; the trade required a currency and one evolved; the currency went online; and now it trades against the dollar at a fairly constant per-unit cost of a little more than a dollar. The story of Magic shows how easily almost anything can become money in the Information Age.

In the 1990s, a game of Magic looked like this: two people, usually male nerds, sat across from each other at a card table.[6] Each had a deck of sixty cards. On his turn, Nerd 1 would take one card from the top of his deck. He then played cards from his hand onto the table. Each card had a different effect, such as attacking the other player's life force or destroying one of the other player's cards. Then Nerd 2 drew a card and played some from his hand onto the table. This went on until one player's life points, which start at twenty, were reduced to zero, at which point the game ended.

This simple mechanic—draw and play—is seen in hundreds of card games the world over. Yet Magic became explosively popular through two innovations. First, the rules are not in a rulebook—*they are on the cards*. When you draw a card from your deck, you read what it does. You can then strategize about what to do with it. A card can do very complicated things, but so long as the card tells you exactly what those things are, you don't have to worry about memorizing a bunch of arcane rules. It's all strictly need-to-know! If you don't have a card, its rules don't matter. If you do have it, its rules are right in front of you. The second innovation is that players can build their own decks, buying a specific set of cards from among those printed by the company based on how different sets of cards work together in creative and unexpected ways. Your prowess as a player is a matter in part of luck and in-game play, but also of managing and building a deck with just the right cards. The cards could be acquired by buying packs from the company, like baseball cards, or they could be picked up in trades with other players. Think Fantasy Football on steroids: you are trying to build a "team" of sixty cards that will work well together no matter what team they face.

These innovations allowed Magic to become an intricate and deeply strategic game. In 1994 it was selected as a Mensa Award winner. Yet kids can play it, too. Take a card, read what it does, use it. The brilliance comes in not at the level of reading and implementing cards but in anticipating the flow of cards into your hand and preparing for them. Young children might not do that, nor do they need to. But Einstein and Oppenheimer could have had a great deal of fun with Magic, each knowing exactly what was in his deck, each judging the probability of such-and-such a card being drawn within the next five rounds, the probability of some killer card being drawn before the match was 45 percent finished, and so on. For the very best Magic players, the game is all about how they build their decks to create the possibility of overwhelming combinations of powers.

Here's an example of how the Magic system leads to deck building and card trading. Magic players often characterize their decks by colors, because cards of similar colors tend to work together well. Let's take a green deck as a beginning concept. Green decks are filled with big monsters—large, powerful creatures that do lots of damage when played. Being so large and powerful, however, these monsters require quite a lot of resource build-up, in the form of "mana," before they can be summoned to battle. Therefore a green deck player spends the first half of a match in a very weak state, building up mana slowly. Once he has enough mana, the green guy can unleash his horde of Bears, Rhinos, and Spiders on the enemy, wiping him out. This strategy is different from what a player with a red deck would employ. Red cards tend to involve instant, small damage. A red player sends waves of little creeps to pick off life points here and there from his enemy. When red plays green, the red player hopes his creeps can take down the green player early, before the latter can build up enough power to bring out his massive goons.

Most tournament play in Magic, however, is done with decks combining blue and white. White cards preserve and defend life points. Blue cards allow deck management, and this power, more than any, is valued by the best players. A typical blue card allows a player to dig through his deck to find a certain card and put it in play immediately. In other words, he doesn't have to draw the card—he can go get it. Other blue cards let players bring powerful cards back from the discard pile, or to order the next ten cards to be drawn, and so on. If Einstein played Magic, he would play blue/white. His white cards would keep him alive, and his blue cards, combined with his knowledge of probability and card synergies, would allow him to ensure that he had maximal power in hand at all times.

Given these strategies, the cards produced by the company may have greater or lesser value. If I am a red player going up against a green, a card that destroys green mana is extremely valuable to me. If I can put several of these cards in my deck, chances are I will draw one early. If so, I can kill the green guy's mana early, and so set back the timetable of his juggernaut of behemoths. A blue/white player finds any deck-delving card to be very valuable. He puts only a few powerful cards in his deck and then relies on his abilities to dive into the deck to find them. If there's a card that lets him repeatedly go in and grab his most powerful cards, that card would be worth quite a lot in terms of its contribution to his deck's overall power.

Markets naturally emerge from such a situation. And a market did emerge, because Magic was an instant hit. Though originally conceived as a time-waster for fans waiting around for events at game conventions, by 1999 it was itself an event. The publisher, Wizards of the Coast, began releasing new cards at regular intervals. Magic tournaments began to offer prizes in five figures.

All of this made good money for the game's developers. Think about the business model. You've got 100,000 supersmart guys wanting to beat down their friends, and they can buy playing cards to do it. How much would they pay for a slightly better card than the ones currently in their deck? How much does it cost to design and release a single card? This is easy money in the short run: if the average power of existing cards in the system is 5, just invent some funky rule that gives your card a power of 6, pay an artist $100 for a nice image, print and sell. In a world of 5s, who wouldn't pay $1 to have a 6? Or $2? Or $20?

In the long run you have to be more careful. The developers are monopolists and, as we all remember from Econ 101, monopolists understand that they need to restrict their output in order to keep the demand price high. So Magic's developers release new packs, with new rules and powers, only once a year, adding new rules and new powers while "retiring" old packs, making them no longer acceptable for official play, in order to keep a steady demand for new product.

Magic quickly grew to involve thousands of cards with thousands of different powers. The infinite breadth of human creativity expressed itself in the infinite variety of decks people built. Each player had a preferred flavor of deck.

And then came trade. If hundreds of thousands of players all have different tastes, and if the cards are released in random packs, then players have an incentive to exchange cards. It began with barter among kids—I'll give you a Doom Angel for your Forest Lurker. But barter is inefficient. The second kid says, "Wait. Forest Lurker is way more powerful. Give me a Fire Goblin too." And so it goes, with kids: they work it out. Not so the advanced players, who know that Forest Lurker is worth (1.13) × (Doom Angel + Fire Goblin) and thus not a fair trade. These players require a divisible currency, such as the dollar, to facilitate trades, so that Forest Lurker might be worth $2.60 and (Doom Angel + Fire Goblin) $2.30. Once that currency is established, you can make the trade, then throw in thirty cents to make it even.

EBay was an early answer to the demand for card trading in Magic. Even today I can try to buy Isolated Chapel for $11.38 on eBay (nine bids).[7] The only difficulty is the service fees and the hassle. Cards have to be shipped, with attendant costs. Moreover, a fellow involved in this business owes income tax and sales tax; things traded in dollars are subject to the laws and regulations of dollar-land. If you use credit cards, fees have to be paid. It's all very clunky.

There's nothing like the internet to remove clunkiness from a human interaction system, and sure enough in 2002 the company launched an internet-based version of the game, Magic the Gathering Online. The developers designed a client software program that goes onto your home computer and allows you to talk to a central server. Among other functions, the central server sells you digital versions of cards, keeps track of which players have which digital cards, and maintains chat channels in which you can "buddy" another player and then trade cards with him. You can sign up for events: dates and times when many players will come online to play with other members of the network. To sign up for these events, you must pay $1 to the company for a digital admission certificate called an Event Ticket. If you don't use a ticket for the event you originally bought it for, you can store it, give it to another player, or exchange it for other things, such as cards. Or dollars.

Now suppose I want to create a wonderful Magic deck and am willing to pay a lot of money for it. I can go the face-to-face route: search on eBay, buy up all the great cards I can, dutifully paying my sales taxes (or not), and take the risk of not getting my cards in the mail after I've paid. Then I have to find other people to play, go to tournaments in the physical world, and hope for the best.

Or I can do it digitally: head to Magic the Gathering Online, or MtGO, buy a thousand Tickets, and use them to buy the best digital card deck available. No taxes or tax fraud, since the IRS doesn't regard Tickets as money. And I can rely on the company to make the database switch that records the transfer of the card—no worries about stuff getting lost in the mail.[8] It happens instantly, too. Finally, I can find players all the time, online. I just have to keep a few Tickets so I can get into events.

Do the Tickets have real-world value? Yes. As I mentioned, on the day of this writing Tickets are on offer from a third-party supplier at $1.04 each.[9] When you think about it, this is rather shocking. Why should Tickets sell on the open market for *more* than a dollar, when anyone can log in and buy them directly from the company for $1 each? The reason, of course, is that purchases from the company are taxable. In much of Europe, Value Added Tax (VAT) rates exceed 20 percent. Sales taxes in most U.S. states are above 5 percent. Players who are subject to these tax rates would naturally prefer to pay $1.04 to a third party than $1.08, say, to a combination of the game developer and the government.

This does not explain why a Ticket's value on the open market would be anywhere near $1. Imagine: You have a business that consists of an Excel spreadsheet. In the spreadsheet is a very long list of names, and next to the names is a column of numbers, which you have labeled "Tickets." You send an email to each of these people saying, "I will increase the number listed under 'Tickets' if you send me $1." Assume that for some unknown reason, lots of people actually send you the money. How much does it cost you to change numbers in a database? Basically nothing. Yet you get $1 each time you do it. As the owner of this business and a person wanting to drive fancy cars, your first impulse is to perform this "service" as many times as requested! Whatever the source of demand, your first impulse is to satisfy it by spewing out Tickets as rapidly as possible. If you're selling lemonade that costs you nothing to make, and people are paying $1 a cup, you want to push all the lemonade you can. But pushing out lots of product can lower the demand—eventually you get to the point where everybody's got some Tickets, and no one wants to pay $1 for more. Well, fine: charge $0.90. You'll get some more customers and $0.90 is still above your cost, which is $0. When that well runs dry, you can lower the price again, to $0.80, and so on all the way down. Your gut tells you to push product out the door so long as you can charge more for it than it costs you.

The Monopolist in Econ 101, however, understands that you make more money by keeping the market value high. The people who run Magic understand this, and they limit the number of cards they release. They also do things to sustain Ticket values. They don't limit the release of Tickets, but they do keep a steady price of $1. The company then shores up demand for Tickets among third parties by holding events that require large numbers of Tickets. In the early days, you needed one Ticket to play in an event. Today, some events cost thirty Tickets to enter. Some mandarin deep within the bowels of the Wizards of the Coast office building, call him the Magic Central Banker (Alan Nerdspan?), watches the supply and demand for Tickets and issues recommendations to the people running events on what prices to charge. If he decides that the open-market price of the Ticket is too low, he tells the company to raise the Ticket cost of events. If it is too high, he tells them to lower the event Ticket price. By these methods, the Magic Central Banker can keep the market value of Magic Tickets near $1.

The people who run Magic the Gathering apparently believe monetary stability is a good thing. The open-market price of Tickets has stayed within a fairly narrow band, from $0.80 to $1.20. This value stability leads to another surprise: the existence of profit-seeking companies in this market. Magic has some 300,000 registered players, creating a lot of potential for trade. Cardhoarder.com, for example, makes its money buying and selling cards and Tickets.[10] It has programmed "bots," fake players, to help with trading. Cardhoarder registers an account on the MtGO site and gives its fake player a name like "Cardhoarder Card Buy Bot." The bot is then programmed to communicate with human players within a fairly narrow protocol, involving things like listing a bunch of cards and stating their prices, or offering to buy cards from players for a certain number of Tickets. At its website, the company simply says "Check out our bots online!" On the website you can pay

Cardhoarder real money to obtain "Bot Credits." When you then talk to the bot in the system, it will tell you how many Bot Credits you have. You can ask to see card prices in terms of Tickets or in Bot Credits. You can pay sellers through the website in Tickets, Dollars, or Euros. Cardhoarder is just one of a cottage industry of companies involved in streamlining the movement of cards, Tickets, and dollars through the world of Magic the Gathering Online.

None of this private activity would be feasible if the Ticket value fluctuated crazily. Its existence speaks to the stability of these markets and the robustness of the items traded. Hordes of users casually trade dollars for bits and back again with complete confidence.

Is there a bright line here between the real and virtual economies? I don't see one. Are Tickets play money? Yes, if "play money" means money that makes sense only in a game; no, if "play money" means something that cannot have any dollar value. The right answer in this case is yes *and* no, which only proves that the concept of *play money* is fishy. The reason Tickets exist is that they are tax-advantaged. If this is permissible, why isn't Amazon allowed to use a virtual currency for its operations? Why can't we all use play money all the time?

A final twist: if you buy a complete set of MtGO digital cards, you can pay the company a nominal fee and it will destroy your online cards and send you the print version. Thus you can pay someone in Tickets to get their digital cards, then redeem the digital cards into paper cards for face-to-face play. In other words, you can use play money—Tickets—to buy something real: Magic cards. The virtual values of the Magic economy thus leak slowly but inexorably into the real world.

EVE ONLINE

EVE Online, founded in 2003, is one of the longest-running online games today. The game takes place in a brutally Hobbesian environment in which mafia-like groups of players, called "corporations," make merciless war on one another. Anyone not part of a corp is fodder. All of this is by design, because the founders of EVE are devotees of Ayn Rand and view freedom, competition, and property as the cornerstones of the ideal society.

Rand's theories are in many ways confirmed by the experience of EVE Online. The players who survive there have earned a reputation for elite performance and strategic wisdom. There are no rules, no laws, and no courts. Fraud, intimidation, and extortion are all acceptable business strategies. In this environment, some corps rise to the top and seize vast areas of space, where they make their own law. Despite having no real-world connections to one another, the players in the corps sustain long-run trust relationships, often lasting several years. In a no-holds-barred competitive galaxy, survivors are very able.

Given their ideological commitments, it is unsurprising that EVE's designers adopted no particular policy regarding the practice of selling game currency for real money. When EVE was launched, however, the game industry was embroiled in a bitter debate on this topic. Should you let players trade game gold for dollars, or not? Most online games had an in-game currency: credits, gold pieces, doubloons, and so on, which some players would accumulate in large stores. They then might decide that they had much more than they needed. Or perhaps they were going to quit the game.

In either case, you had some players with game money they didn't need. Other players, meanwhile, had too little. They could use game money to enhance their power by buying better weapons and armor and so on. Some of those players might be well-off in real-world terms relative to the veteran players with their unneeded game money. Thus a market opportunity emerged: if dollar-poor veteran players sold game money to dollar-rich players, both parties would be better off. The dollar-rich players got more in-game playing power, and the veteran players got real-world spending power.

The means of trading is straightforward: A veteran player posts a for-sale ad on the internet (perhaps on eBay, perhaps on a site dedicated to real-money trade). The ad lists what currency is for sale, how much, and what dollar price is demanded. It also states terms of delivery, as in "After I receive your check for $100, I will meet you in-game in front of the White Palace in Camelot and turn the gold pieces over to you there."

When EVE was born, some companies opposed this practice while others supported it; we will look more closely at real-money trading in a later chapter. For now, what matters is that EVE Online was quite happy that its game currency was being traded by players for real currency. EVE's in-game currency was called ISK, which happens to be the official abbreviation of Iceland's official currency, the Icelandic krona. Let the other shoe drop: EVE Online's development company, CCP, is based in Reykjavik.

The economy was always, and remains, a central element of gameplay. EVE's galaxy is vast; it takes several hours to cross from one side to the other. There are thousands of stars, thousands of planets, and tens of thousands of places to go. Going places requires a ship. Ships often get blown up (usually by other players). To keep a presence in the world, you need to have a hangar with several ships inside. Keeping your fleet intact requires that you constantly buy new ships. New ships are built by players and sold on open markets.

To build a ship, you need blueprints and components. Components are things like shields, propulsion units, navigation systems, and guns. If you want to build a mining ship, you give it huge cargo bays and powerful engines. A truck, basically. Like real-world trucks, mining vessels are slow, vulnerable, and poorly armed. But they can haul stuff. Alternatively, you could build a scout ship. It might have fast engines, a decent weapon, some armor, and a cloaking device. Or you could build a cruiser: fast, medium armor, with powerful torpedoes, lasers, and guns. There's an endless variety of ships to build.

Putting together a ship and its components requires all kinds of resources. The basic resource is rock ("ore"). You find rock in asteroids. For a new player, the best way to start is to get a small mining ship and sneak out to asteroids, mine them for ore, then carry the ore to populated space stations and sell it. With your profits, you buy a bigger mining ship, and repeat. Or you can get a large cargo vessel and play the markets, taking advantage of small price differences between planets. Perhaps one type of ore is cheap in a certain sector because over the past week the miners have found a lot of it. Yet the shipbuilders in this other sector tire of having to run over there constantly for new inputs, and have bid up the price of ore in their own sector. Voilà, a delivery opportunity emerges! Buy the ore in the mining sector and sell it in the production sector for a profit. You only have to dodge the pirates, players who lurk along the route and demand payment for safe passage.

When being a trucker becomes boring, the enterprising EVE player can engage directly in arbitrage. As a player advances, he can choose to enhance certain skills. Skills can take anywhere from five minutes to ten days to learn; to learn a skill, you simply click "Learn Skill," and when the time is up, you have that skill. While many players beef up their combat and navigation skills, there are paths for commercially oriented players as well. Trade skills allow a player to see more and more data about prices in faraway markets. Advanced trading skills let the player place buy and sell orders all over the galaxy.

For EVE traders (and there are a lot of them), game play consists of opening multiple spreadsheets listing items and prices in widely distributed planetary systems. The trader scans these spreadsheets for arbitrage opportunities, places where the current sell price significantly exceeds the current buy price.[11] The trader places a buy order just above the current buy price, and waits. Generally another player will take the buy order; when that happens, the trader finds himself with inventory. He then places a sell order for the inventory at a price just below the current sell price. If another player takes the sell order, the trader has made a profit equal to a bit less than the original bid-ask spread.

Why do these arbitrage opportunities exist? They exist because most players focus on combat skills, not trade skills. They cannot see all the markets. Nor can they place buy/sell orders for their gear anywhere in the galaxy, like characters with high trade skills can.

Thus it often happens that a combat player, a pirate, pulls into dock with a load of loot for which he sees just one price, the buy price of a single trader. His choice is to sell his stash right then and there, taking the cash, or drive around to different planets and stations in the hope of getting a better price before he is blown to smithereens by another pirate. Many simply take the money. Similarly, a pirate looking for a fast upgrade to his guns may pull into a station and see only a few items on display for purchase. His choice is to pay the local price or to go shopping. Many simply pay and head back to battle. Traders who pull into these stations, however, get to see a full readout of all buy/sell offers on all goods, in many nearby planetary systems. This information allows the trader to find opportunities for profit that other players cannot see.

EVE's developers have created these arbitrage opportunities on purpose, by restricting trading information to players who have purchased the required skills. As a result of this design, EVE is the most market-driven game in existence. Playing the game involves buying and selling the things you need on the game's markets. Almost everything in the game can be purchased for ISK. ISK, in turn, can be earned in-game or purchased from other players. It is not unusual for a new player to spend $10, $20, or $100 to buy ISK that can be used to outfit a new fleet of ships for combat, hauling, or survival. Trade in ISK has continued for many years with no major crashes or booms. EVE's ISK behaves in many respects like a real currency. The Wikipedia page for the real-world ISK, the Icelandic krona, is even forced to include a disambiguation statement: " 'ISK' redirects here. For the currency of the Eve Online video game, see Gameplay of Eve Online#Economy."[12]

EVE was evidently designed by people who understand markets. As you make your way through most online games, you frequently have to buy and sell things. Usually, this involves going up to a nonplayer person or box labeled "Merchant" or some such, clicking on it, and doing your buying or selling. In EVE, doing this (with a trader character) gives you a list of all outstanding buy and sell orders within a large radius. You can track prices over time, through different moving averages that you specify. Your screen looks like that of a Wall Street trader or a currency arbitrager. These are real live markets.

The free trading of ISK against the dollar creates a point of contact with the real economy. There's no reason why a person could not hold wealth in the form of ISK, turning it into real money only as necessary. One could also launder money: sell dirty dollars for ISK, then use the ISK to buy clean dollars. The only limit is scale. At its height, EVE's player population is perhaps thirty thousand. In one sense this is a large number: imagine an entire town "living" in a cyberspace environment that replicates a genuine space environment. And they're doing this twenty-four hours a day, seven days a week. EVE is always on. But in a global sense, thirty thousand people is small potatoes.

EVE is best considered a small, perfect example of what online spaces can be when the designers think very hard about creating free spaces. It's a libertarian's paradise. Almost every significant player experience is mediated by a free market. Other player organizations are completely emergent, simply agreements among free people to act in certain ways. The entire social system is enforced only by the people within it. EVE powerfully represents a specific vision of what life can be. It tells us that online life in the future will present us with all kinds of visions about society: socialist, religious, technophile, literary. Each will have its own approach to markets, and its own currency.

FACEBOOK

Facebook is a huge social network program, made even more famous by the film *The Social Network*. By "huge" I mean lots of active users, more than 1 billion as of this writing and still growing.

If Facebook were a country, it would be a big one. The United States has about 320 million people. China and India each have more than 1 billion. Facebook's "population" dwarfs those of lands like Russia, Brazil, and Indonesia. If something truly significant ever happens in Facebook, it will affect quite a lot of people.

What does happen in Facebook? It began as a digital copy of the freshman introduction books that some U.S. colleges give out to new students. A new student doesn't know anyone. How handy, to have a list of faces and names, so you could look up that guy with the nice smile you met at the orientation social. Facebook is a list of faces and names on steroids, the added punch coming from the affordances of digital technology. With digital technology, it's easy to add details like hometown, club memberships, interests, opinions. It's also easy to link these items, showing who is friends with whom, belongs to what club, or shares what opinion. It's easy to embed different kinds of information: audio, video, graphics, apps. It's easy to allow messaging. The easiest thing of all is that users do this themselves. Facebook itself makes no content at all. It is simply a platform for people to post things and connect them.

Both the posted things and the connections are content; they have value to the site's users, a value that grows according to the principles of network economics.[13] The first telephone ever invented was useless. The second not only had some positive value but gave the first one value too. The third phone added value to the first and second: now there were two places you could call instead of one. And so on. When the utility of a good depends on how many other people have it, its value to each person rises as more people get the good. Facebook has this property. All those users uploading and tagging and linking and messaging provide valuable information to everyone on the site.

There are, of course, limits. Facebook reports that it has one billion "active users," but a little perspective on this concept might be helpful. When I first joined Facebook, in 2007, it billed itself as a semiexclusive website for university students. It seemed appropriate for a forward-looking, techno-savvy professor (basically, "a guy too old to really be a nerd") to jump in. Within a few weeks, however, I realized two things. First, Facebook creates a lot of work. When you're more closely connected to more people who want your time, you have more things to do. Second, Facebook loves having all the data about me that my "friends" and I love to upload. Facebook's use is usually commercial, but there are social-reputational issues. Suppose I have a few too many at the department holiday party and a "friend" takes a picture of me with a lampshade on my head. My "friend" puts the picture on his own Facebook page and tags it with my name and some nice caption like "Here's Ted being an asshole!!!!" From that moment and forevermore, the picture will be part of my Facebook photo album. It's true that this could have happened on the web itself, before Facebook came along. But Facebook made the essential elements of building a personal website (pictures, opinions, links) trivially easy.

When I realized that Facebook membership was akin to being life-logged by "friends," I decided to opt out. It was not easy. You cannot cancel your Facebook account. It's free, so you can't stop paying to make the account go away. You can go to a webpage and click a "cancel" button, but that does not erase your Facebook page. It took a phone call to Facebook customer service to make that happen. Even so, Facebook constantly reaches out at you; everyone you meet sends Facebook-originated emails inviting you to become their friend on the site. Finally, in 2011, after years of resistance, I succumbed. A game was being published as a Facebook app, and the only way to get into the game was to join Facebook. On returning, I was appalled to discover that every single byte of information that had been there in 2007 was still there in 2011. I signed in using the same username and password, and my site appeared as if it had never been gone. Like a digital Rip Van Winkle, I had active friend requests from four years earlier, still patiently awaiting my response. It was as if my membership had never lapsed.

We should bear this story in mind when considering Facebook's population numbers. According to Facebook's statistics page, it seems that "active user" refers only to people who have an account.[14] The site claims that more than 50 percent of these users do log into their account on a given day. Even so, these logins represent a very wide distribution pattern of use. Some people are there simply to play a time-wasting game for a few minutes. Others rely on the site to maintain their social lives. There is anecdotal evidence of "Facebook fatigue," of people getting tired of being contacted out of the blue by folks they knew (and are now embarrassed to have known) decades before. Social networks create connections, but connections require maintenance. There are limits on the impact of Facebook in any one person's life, and on Facebook's global impact.

Another sign of Facebook's limitations is that it is not actually a universal network. If you happen to live in a Facebook-dominated country, it might seem that everyone in the world must be on it. But networks, like languages, can create walls of resistance. In Brazil, many people still use Orkut, a predecessor to Facebook (like Myspace and Friendster). China's biggest social network is Qzone; Facebook is banned. In Russia, the site V Kontake gets more hits than YouTube, Google, or Facebook.[15]

This discussion is an important preface to an unquestionably true statement: Facebook has an economy. It has production, markets, trade, and currency. Much of it is driven by the system of Facebook applications, a technology by which developers can create applications that run on Facebook as a platform. An application operating as a game might allow people to "produce" digital carrots that other people can then buy to "feed" their digital bunnies. Each of these elements operates in a pretty normal way.

What is definitely *not* normal is the emergence, within a single decade, of a completely new economy of a billion people. That doesn't happen often in history; economists are not sure it has ever happened. It may not have happened now. Facebook, though a genuine economy, may not be a significant one. It is hard to tell. Facebook is a virtual economy, weirdly normal like the rest. Mostly, it raises a lot of difficult questions.

Let's begin with the money. In 2010, Facebook had money, a currency called the "Facebook Credit" or cc. There was no open market in cc against the dollar, because Facebook did not allow users to simply transfer cc to one another. Instead, you paid Facebook for cc, at the rate of 10 for $1, and could use them to pay for virtual goods and currencies inside Facebook apps and games. The people who develop and own these apps and games would then redeem the credits from Facebook for seven cents each. That is, Facebook charged users ten cents for credits, but paid just seven cents to app developers when it bought the credits back.[16] It forbade anyone from trading cc with others. Moreover, those who accepted cc in their Facebook apps were not allowed to provide any tangible item or service in return. To enforce these terms, Facebook reserved the right to kick a developer out of the credits system at its sole discretion.

This all came to end in June 2012. Rather than turn the cc into an actual currency, Facebook chose instead to create a payments system. Users of Facebook apps who wish to buy virtual items now do it using real currencies. Facebook simply stands ready to manage these real-money trades. It takes the user's payment information and charges it accordingly, and then assigns the appropriate number of virtual items or currencies to the user's account. Facebook gives the real money to the application developer at seventy cents on the dollar. The structure of payments is the same, but now there is no platform-wide currency. Instead, the platform seamlessly translates between local real currencies and virtual currencies and items. There is no reason to have a Facebook Credit to translate among currencies. The digital system does it.

Here's an example of how the Facebook system works. Let's say I have a company called Bob's Games. Here at Bob's Games, we make digital games that run in web browsers. Our hottest game is called Barnyard. In Barnyard, players are chickens that run around trying to peck up little seeds while being chased by a wolf. The more you peck, the more powerful your chicken gets. When your chicken gets superpowerful, it can peck bigger stuff. At first, it's bigger seeds. Then it's other chickens. At some point, you can peck up the wolves, then the farm, then the town. Each time you peck something bigger, you get more power, which lets you peck something bigger still. Of course, to keep the game interesting, the game provides bigger predators that are harder and harder to avoid. The final phase of the game has you pecking entire continents and planets, while fending off massive alien chicken-hunting enemies, until your chicken becomes master of the universe.

From beginning to end, Barnyard can take weeks to play. You start as a humble Rhode Island Red and end as Super Chicken of the Universe; that takes a lot of pecking. It's a grind of sorts but somehow entertaining. We at Bob's Games know that. We made the game that way on purpose, because some people who want to become Super Chicken of the Universe, and don't want to grind through all that pecking, will pay money to peck faster. We offer the game for free, to get people hooked on pecking and growing their chicken. But then we offer them little enhancements, like Super Chicken Feed that doubles the power you get from pecking. We let them build better barnyards with stronger fences, to keep the bigger wolves out. We let them set their chicken on Auto-Peck™, so that it grows a little even when players are not logged in. In a final coup, we let people with big chickens send gifts to people with little chickens, to help them out.

For Bob's Games, Facebook is a great platform. We put Barnyard in Facebook and used the friend feature to determine who could send Barnyard gifts to whom. We also established an in-game market. We made up a currency, the Peckle, and let people use it to buy and sell different kinds of seeds. We created different chicken types with different colors, and let people raise a whole flock of chickens at once. But each chicken needs a different kind of seeds. People can grow the seeds, but each Barnyard can only grow one type. So if you want to raise different chickens, you have to grow a lot of your own seed type and then sell the excess for Peckles. You then use your Peckles to buy the seeds you need. Or, if you want to grow faster, you can just buy your Peckles from us directly.

Being on Facebook means that you can't send Bob's Games your money in return for Peckles. You have to buy your Peckles from Facebook. When we launched Barnyard in early 2012, you would buy Facebook Credits from Facebook, and then spend the credits in our store to buy Peckles and whatever other virtual items you wanted (seeds, chickens, and barnyard upgrades). Now you buy Peckles directly from Facebook, and you can spend them in our store. Both systems work out the same way: Facebook gets dollars, you get virtual items, and we get 70 percent of the money you paid Facebook.

About once a month, we redeem our revenues balance with Facebook. Last month we picked up 100,000 Peckles from chicken lovers. These Peckles cost our players $10,000 to buy, of which we cleared $7,000 after Facebook deducted its service fee. The players got 100,000 Peckles of chicken-gaming fun, and Facebook netted $3,000.

Most Facebook apps operate the same way. They provide some sort of virtual good or service and charge real money for it; the money goes to Facebook; and Facebook remits 70 percent to the developer. Note that none of the economic activity within the Facebook app itself appears in the official economic statistics of the real world. The real world sees only that the internet company reported income of $10,000 and expenses of $7,000, while the game company reported income of $7,000. The Peckles and seeds and chickens and barnyard upgrades are all invisible to the outside world. Yet they have economic value beyond the $10,000 paid into the Facebook system. Users paid $10,000 to get certain virtual items, but they got other virtual items for free. Recall that in Barnyard you can enhance your chicken without buying anything. Anyone can build a Super Chicken of the Universe without paying a dime in real money. That chicken has economic value. In the game its value is expressed in Peckles, but it could just as easily be expressed in dollars and yen. The value exists.

Wait. Bob's Games' virtual chickens have value? Of course they do. They took human time to create. They are valued by their users. They are persistent; the virtual chicken lasts weeks longer than most cheeseburgers. Other items in the Facebook economy provide unquestionably valuable services, such as reducing the time it takes a person to do something. Never mind that what she is doing is growing an intangible chicken. That doesn't mean the service is economically unimportant. People try to do all kinds of strange things and receive all kinds of strange services, yet we do not strike these services out of the national accounting statistics because they are weird. The Central Statistical Office does not separate the Weird and Normal Economies. Every year, Americans spend untold billions of dollars on shirts and hats that have a certain sports team logo sewn on. They could just buy a red shirt, but they will pay significantly more for a red shirt with a big white interlocked I and U on it (the symbol of my university, which I paid for and wear). We do not strike the cost of sewing on the IU symbol out of the GDP. It is not the economist's job to declare whether products and services are sensible or meaningful. The economist's job is simply to record what people buy and how much time and money industry expends providing it. From that perspective, there exists inside Facebook a hidden economy that is unobserved, unregulated, untaxed, and unmanaged—except by Facebook itself.

None of this would matter if Facebook were just a little game. Think of Monopoly, one of the world's most popular games. Like Facebook, it has money, markets, and trading. Like Facebook, it's all virtual. Why doesn't Monopoly game playing raise eyebrows? For starters, Monopoly is played by four people for an hour. It doesn't last. When the game is over, the money you made and the assets you bought instantly lose their value. The rules prohibit you from starting a Monopoly game with money and properties you got last time. They also prohibit you from using the dollars in your wallet to buy things. Monopoly assets don't trade against anything outside the world of the game, and the world of the game is ephemeral.

Facebook is like an endless Monopoly game played by a billion people. The assets last, and they trade, directly or indirectly, for assets in the real world. Facebook monies are exchanged for dollars all the time. And the items and services they pay for can persist for years.

The only question, again, is whether Facebook is an important economy. No one (to my knowledge) has calculated its value. Only Facebook could do it; only the company can accurately gauge the value of all the items and services being traded. We do have estimates of Facebook's revenue from virtual item sales, which was about $800 million annually in 2012 and rising rapidly.[17] But this figure represents just the growth in the money supply. In 2010, the U.S. money supply was about $1.8 trillion. But the economy produced more than $14 trillion in new goods and services (the gross domestic product, or GDP) in this period.[18] In other words, the GDP was almost eight times the money supply. If this ratio also applies to the Facebook economy, then the $800 million money supply would suggest a Facebook GDP of $6.2 billion.

The GDP of Barbados is right around $4 billion.[19] Thus Facebook right now may have an economy the size of a small and pretty island. But unlike that island, Facebook's economy can grow and grow and grow.

And the normal weirdness of Facebook is beginning to trickle into the real economy. Facebook's terms of service strictly prohibit anyone from selling tangible products for virtual ones. By "tangible," it means objects that can be physically delivered to a consumer. But what does "physical" mean? You have to use muscles? You can deliver an awful lot of stuff to a consumer without using anybody's muscles. In March 2011, Warner Brothers announced it would rent movies via Facebook.[20] Miramax followed in August.[21]

Also in 2011, Facebook launched a new service called Deals. Go to Facebook on your smartphone and the service will give you a list of local businesses offering promotions. Tap the promotion and show your phone to the cashier to receive either 20 percent off or two items for the price of one. Facebook has begun by offering this service to businesses for free, but one can imagine that its long-term plan may be different. However the Deals program develops, it will almost certainly involve lubrication by Facebook payments. The virtual money we earn on Facebook may become an alternate form of payment for burgers and fries, oil changes, and soap. Nothing's more real than burgers and fries, especially if more than a billion people are being served.

STEAM

Steam is a game distribution channel for personal computers. Around the turn of the century, the game developer Valve faced the problem of how best to update its games. A computer game is a piece of software; it can always be improved and in some cases it must be improved to succeed in its marketplace. Before the internet had penetrated deeply into society, the standard model of game software development was "fire and forget," that is, develop software to a certain state, then sell it. If it failed, it failed. Improvements, if any, would come only with the next version of the game, which would also be developed and released as is. There was no capacity for removing bugs or regularly updating the program.

This changed with the advent of internet-only games such as Ultima Online and EverQuest. These games existed only on servers and were played remotely by users through a local client. The game on the server could be changed at any time. If the changes had implications for the client, such as alterations to art files or locally executed game rules, then a "patch" could be created. Clients would be updated on the fly with new game content and rules. It became common for a game to be developed and released in a somewhat buggy state, then repeatedly patched and improved after release.

Valve's most popular online game was a multiplayer shooter called Counter-Strike. It was a fairly small game, involving a few rules, art assets, weapons, and maps. Keeping it fresh meant implementing new maps and features fairly frequently. This required frequent patching to all the players' computers, which involved Valve in the problem of building a patching protocol. The Steam patching system appeared in 2002 and was required for those who wished to play Counter-Strike—at the time, a population of several hundred thousand.

Because Valve had several online games, Steam was conceived as a general system for feeding game code and assets to a large number of players. As such, it was also suitable as a digital distribution platform for new games. Players could use Steam not just to obtain new content for games they already owned but to acquire files for new games. In 2005, Steam began to host new games developed by third parties. To allow those games to be sold and not just given away, Valve added a payment system to Steam.

Steam thus became a one-stop shop for buying new games as well as patching, revising, and extending current games. At the time, games, like movies and music, were moving to a digital distribution model. With Steam, there is no need to go to the mall or to Amazon .com. No physical media are ever created. I simply sign into my

Steam client, browse to a game I would like to play, and click "Buy."
In moments the game is downloaded and ready to go on my PC.
Steam has become incredibly popular; as I write in early 2013, it is
being used by 5.7 million players.

The story of Steam to 2010: a company makes a platform for
distributing digital content and sells that content for real money. So
far, nothing weird.

Now consider Steam Workshop, Valve's latest innovation in
digital distribution. Workshop enables user-generated content sales.
User-generated content, or UGC, has been an element of online
games for almost as long as virtual currency. The earliest UGC was
in the form of mods, modifications to a game that were made by the
users. Once one user modifies the game, the modification can be
given or sold to others. Some games evolved extended communities
of modders, with websites hosting thousands of game elements for
free use. The mods might involve new rules, new equipment, new
locations, or new characters. Some games were largely popular only
as modified by UGC. The Sims franchise gained much of its popu-
larity from the way it enabled users to make new things and share
them. Second Life is an online virtual world built entirely from UGC.
Valve's Counter-Strike began life as a user-built mod of the company's single-player shooter game Half-Life.

The only problem with UGC from an industry standpoint is
monetization. If a company makes a platform for content developed
by users, how does it make money? If you are Facebook, you do it
with ads and by selling the copious amounts of users' personal data.
These options are not as lucrative for a game company; ads interfere
with the immersion necessary for games to be entertaining, and game

companies as a rule do not learn very much about their users' consumer preferences. If a company tried to claim ownership of user-generated content, the content stream would dry up. The stream has to be fairly large to be worth anything; one rule of thumb for UGC is that 99 percent of it is garbage.

How then does a company make money from the UGC generated by its games? Steam Workshop has the following model. Users can make anything they want for the games on Steam's systems. They can post these assets on the Steam Workshop page. Other users can browse, filter, and select the content they want. When they have selected new content, the Steam system seamlessly embeds it in the user's game on the system. You don't just choose content on Steam Workshop, you *subscribe* to it. If the content is updated by its maker in the future, Steam will automatically update your game files to reflect the change. In other words, Steam turns UGC into another element of patching and updating. The difference is that the content comes from other users.

The innovation Valve made is not technical but financial. There is a second tab in Steam Workshop, called Market. When a user selects a piece of UGC on Steam Market, he pays for it with real money, which comes from the user's Steam Wallet. The Steam Wallet is accessed through the user's Account page; you can add funds to it by authorizing a charge to your credit card. You can also put money in your Steam Wallet by buying Steam Wallet codes at brick-and-mortar stores like Best Buy. The money in your Steam Wallet can be used to buy games or to buy items in games. But you cannot get it back. According to the terms of the Steam subscriber agreement, you have no rights of ownership over the funds in "your" Steam

Wallet. The money, once transferred into your Steam Wallet, becomes part of a wholly virtual currency under the administration of Valve Inc., not the U.S. government. In the 1990s, Valve was a maker of computer games. Today it is also a financial services company.

When you buy a user-created item on the Steam Workshop, the money comes from you via the Steam Wallet. Where does it go? Most of it is effectively kept by Valve. You paid Valve real money to put virtual dollars into your Steam Wallet, so, in effect, Valve already has all that money, whether you buy user-created gear or not. Valve does not, however, keep all the money, even though it could. Instead it gives a portion of it to the item creator. Valve transfers a real-money balance from its accounts to the creator's account that reflects how often the item sold on the Workshop market. If a person creates a popular virtual item, that person can make quite a bit of real money.

According to Valve company reports, some creators are making a great deal of money by selling content they have made.[22] The system appears to be very successful. At the moment, Valve appears to be aiming for a larger market by building a new console for the television. Having turned PCs into a digital content market, Valve apparently hopes to do the same for TVs.

For now, funds in the Steam Wallet can be used only to buy content on the Steam network. Yet as this network expands from computers to televisions, the amount and variety of purchasable items has no real limit. There's no technical reason why Steam Wallet Dollars (SWD) could not be used to purchase anything currently offered at Amazon.com. There's no technical reason why a person could not offer a service to another person in return for SWD. I could create a blank piece of UGC and use it to advertise my willing-ness to mow lawns for 20 SWD each. There are no practical, tech-nical, or legal constraints preventing the SWD from being used just as dollars are used. Valve simply does not see that as part of its business model. What it will see in a decade, we cannot know. We do know, however, that this company has pushed digital marketing innovation very hard in the past.

WEIRDLY NORMAL

These four cases all play out in ways that economic and business theory can explain. We have firms providing goods and services in the hopes of making a profit. They use the available technology to the best of their ability. They hope to attract business and then monetize it. As a result of these pursuits, markets spring up and trades are conducted.

But nested within this ordinary activity are some odd ducklings. Intangible items that are never traded are nonetheless said to have economic value. People whose training and background are in enter-tainment, not banking, are running huge monetary and financial systems. Silly customer-loyalty program points are treated as balance-sheet items. Social networks are seen as never-ending games among millions of people, so that the play money they manipulate starts to look like real money. This mix of normalcy and oddity invites some reflection. Is anything really happening here?

2

FORMS OF MONEY

I t is a mistake to think of some money as "real" and other money as "fake" or "play" or "virtual." The value of money has always depended on what people think, which is not a "real" thing. Even gold, whose worth is so culturally ingrained that many people are convinced of its inherent value, is useful as money only because people think it is. The disconnect between the properties of the good as a good, and the good as a piece of money, has always been there. Still, money, especially "real" money (by which most people mean the money backed by the state), used to be a lot more real than it is now. Nuggets of metal are at least tangible. Now money consists of database entries, which have no independent value at all and are treated as valuable only because a government says we have to.

Though money has always emerged from social expectations, it is by no means ephemeral or inert. Money exerts a powerful force on human affairs. It is a sign that the invisible hand is moving, and it apparently cannot be stopped. Even in online games, where the designers can control literally everything in the environment, money goes its own way and sometimes offers economy managers nasty surprises. The apparent weirdness of wildcat currency is only apparent. Social media and game money is just the latest manifestation of what money has always been.

A BRIEF HISTORY OF MONEY

When people think of the origin of money, they usually think of a historical process by which paper, backed only the state, replaced metal coins. There's more to it than that.

HARD METAL MONEY

Human trade goes back thousands of years. Stone Age archaeological digs often turn up stones and shells originating hundreds of miles away. How else could they have gotten there except by trade?[1] At some point, people began treating one good as *the* good by which all other goods are counted and measured. A word like "shekel" is now understood to mean a form of money, but originally it was a measure of weight. The pound sterling is of course a measure of weight as well. The worth of all things was measured in terms of the weight of one specific thing, barley in the case of the shekel and silver in the case of the pound.

At first, barley was just one good among many that people bartered. Gradually it became a way to express the value of two different goods: a camel might be worth twelve bushels of barley, but a robe might be worth only one. Finally the proto-money good became the item that people actually used in most exchanges: rather than trade twelve robes for a camel, one traded camels and robes against barley and used one's barley holdings to make up any difference. "Shekel," originally a weight measure for barley, became a general word for the value of things.

Of all the things traded in human prehistory, only a few persistently emerged as *the* money. Camels and barley and rings were occasionally used, but heavy metals had features that made them much more common. Gold, being rare, can express large values with small amounts. You can put a camel's worth of gold in your pocket, but not 12 shekels of barley. I've never tried to make trades with whole grains, but I imagine it's not very efficient. Grains cannot be marked—you can mark their container, but the grains can be separated from their container—and while they can be stored for a long time, they can be eaten by vermin. Camels require constant investments of food to retain their value, and they are not identical: my camel may be worth more than yours, at least until mine gets sick or injured or wanders off. Metal coins have none of these disadvantages. They can be stamped and molded and proved against corruption. They don't decay or get eaten.

What heavy metal money does *not* have is practical use. Barley is very useful: it makes bread that people can eat and beer they can drink. You can't eat gold, or distill it into anything with a kick. It is too soft to make a good blade. You can form it into utensils, but other materials are more practical. Silver also has relatively few mundane uses for an Iron Age culture. The metals that emerged as money were not just rare and heavy but mostly ornamental. Their value was always symbolic. In a sense, then, the history of virtual money goes all the way back to heavy metal money. Gold and silver are largely virtual currencies, objects whose value has little to do with their tangible uses.

Controlling the value of money became an important state function. Kings would take lumps of metal, melt them down, and mold them into discs. Signs of official approval and value were stamped upon them. The stamps were intended to certify that the lump consisted of a certain weight. This was necessary because, once metal became money, money could be melted down and reshaped, sometimes with lesser metals thrown in. Metal money could be debased. People could "clip" coins, trimming off small parts of their edges. A small trim wouldn't be noticed, of course, so the next fellow would take the coin as being worth its full weight. Meanwhile, however, the clippings from many different coins could be gathered and melted, and then restamped as a new coin. (The milled edge on many coins is a relic of the time when milling was a defense against clipping.) All such debasing increases the amount of money in circulation. As money increases, its per-unit value decreases. The authorities constantly opposed such practices, since they lowered the value of their own holdings.

Over centuries, as the amount of trade based on money grew, it became apparent that money was a social animal with a life of its own. Thomas Gresham, a sixteenth-century English financier, noted that if two forms of money were circulating and everyone was forced to treat them as having the same exchange value, only one would stay in the economy—the one whose actual value was lower. This is known as Gresham's Law and is often expressed in the formula "Bad money drives out good." By "good" money here is meant a form of commodity money, such as gold coins, whose stamped value is roughly equal to its actual value in trades. The stamped value is the value of the coin as asserted by the state; the trade value is what that amount of the good, in this case gold, can actually be traded for. A gold coin stamped TEN DOLLARS that can be traded for $10 of bubble gum is "good money." "Bad money"—let's say a silver coin—has TEN DOLLARS stamped on it, but the amount of silver it contains can be traded for only $5 worth of bubble gum. The silver money drives out the gold money because spreading the bad money is profitable. If I have silver coins and my buddy has gold coins, and I ask him to trade coins with me, he has to give me a gold coin in a one-for-one exchange with my silver coin. Each says TEN DOLLARS, and the law says the two coins have the same value. But we both know that he's giving me something worth $10 and I'm giving him something worth $5. If he's smart, he'll avoid making trades like that, and the easiest way to avoid them is to avoid gold coins, or to hoard them. But certainly, don't use them in trades. So long as everyone is forced to accept that a silver coin is worth $10 when it isn't, it will make no sense for anyone to trade using gold coins.

Gresham's Law shows that the money system is a social force with its own drivers and resources. It responds in its own way to the conditions in which it lives. The state can pass laws about money, such as "The relative value of gold and silver shall not change," but money will make its own way around.

These value problems with gold and silver money are important for another reason: they demonstrate that we can't get away from money problems by going back to the Gold Standard or Real Money or Money Backed by Something That Feels Heavy in My Hand. Money made of heavy stuff is no more or less valuable, stable, reliable, or sensible than other kinds. It demands different approaches to management; it is not management free.

The corollary is that there's not much difference between metal money and virtual money. They are both money. They present management puzzles, as money always does. The oddness of virtual money comes from its being money, not from its being virtual.

STRANGE MONEY

The term "odd" could be applied to all kinds of things that have been used as money in the past. The fact that a form of money is strange has never invalidated it as money.

For starters, what could be stranger than using food as money? Yet in many times and places, salt has been money. Salt is almost infinitely divisible; it is dense (though not durable); and in earlier times it was quite rare. Salt also had great value as a spice.

A 2009 report on the website CNBC.com reports on one David Doty, a hobbyist and bank executive who gathers different forms of money from around the world.[2] Doty's collection includes such specimens as Parmigiano cheese, wooden planks, and squirrel pelts. And then there are the Rai stones on the island of Yap. Weighing several tons and made of a material not found on Yap, each stone must be mined on faraway Palau and hauled overseas back home, at great cost of time and risk of life and limb. Once in place on Yap, the stones sit there and simply change ownership as a way to record changes in wealth.

Economists have researched the institutions by which an odd object can become money. In 1945, a Cambridge University student named Richard A. Radford, who had been a prisoner of war, described the emergence of cigarettes as currency in a POW camp. While all prisoners received the same essentials, Radford found, differences in tastes led inevitably to trade. One man wanted more soap, another thicker pants. Most trading was for food. Cigarettes were originally just another item of trade, but they "rose from the status of a normal commodity to that of currency." They served as a convenient unit of account: prisoners used them to express the worth of other commodities. In Radford's camp, which eventually held fifty thousand prisoners from many nations, the cigarette served as an able currency for a surprisingly large economy.

An understanding of money seems to be a natural feature of the human mind. Beginning in the 1960s, behavioral psychologists began to use "token economies" as a form of treatment. The approach is based on the idea that tokens are an easy way to manipulate conditioning. In the token economy mode of treatment, the patient is allowed to exchange tokens for reinforcers such as sweets, cigarettes, and music.[3] Since tokens are not "real," the doctors can create and destroy them at will, raising and lowering the price of behaviors as desired. They can make "bad" choices expensive and "good" ones lucrative. They can apply these rewards instantly, with no delay between action and reward. The method has been extended to other patients, including troubled children. The game/family-management system Chore Wars implements a token economy for the home, in which kids do quests and receive rewards in the form of tokens that can buy the things they want (candy, then videogaming time, then the car).

In the end, "money" is an abstract quality that can be applied to almost anything. Money as such does not exist. There is no commodity or item or concept that must necessarily be money. Rather, the descriptor "money" can be applied to all kinds of different things. The word "money" is like the word "cute." Society applies the concept of cuteness to different things at different times. Not everything is cute, but some things certainly can be. Some things become cute more easily than others. But nothing is necessarily cute. "Cuteness" is simply a property that society puts on things.

Like cuteness, money consists of a set of vague general properties. "Cute" can encompass cuddly, sweet, endearing, charming, small, clean, or happy. The properties of money can be utility for exchange, capacity for value storage, compactness, density, rarity, ease of division, ease of counting, portability. Anything with these features is money. The money-ness is in the features, not in the thing itself.

PAPER MONEY

Nowhere is the inessential nature of the object to which "money" is applied more evident than in the case of paper money. Paper that has already been written on is next to useless, except as a record of whatever was written down. Yet for many centuries now, paper has been a form of money. Before the digital age, it was "the" money.

Paper money has been used by different civilizations at different times over the past several thousand years. Early in its history, paper money was "stuff money" in the sense that it had enough value as a commodity that even a slip of it was worth a little something. Today, however, we think of paper money as money with no commodity value. Although the Chinese and Mongols issued paper money (as fiat money, no less—money declared to have value by power of government alone), paper money became a permanent economic institution only in the Italian Renaissance.

Northern Italy in the Renaissance was a vibrant center of trade. Italian trading houses adopted the practice of issuing bills against the receipt of goods. A bill might indicate that the holder could receive so-and-so many pounds of pepper from the Marco Tullio trading house. Since the bill had implicit value through its connection to the price of pepper, it could be used in exchange. Franco might give this bill to Luca in exchange for something else, such as several pounds of salt. By this practice, the paper bill became a form of money. Its value would be sustained so long as its implied promise was reliable—that is, so long as it could be exchanged for goods of value from the trading house that issued it.

GOLDSMITHS AND NOTES

In the seventeenth century, English goldsmiths took this practice further. Goldsmiths, being in the business of crafting golden objects, developed a capacity for securely storing large amounts of gold. They also followed the practice of issuing bills against the gold they had. Suppose Alfred the merchant brings ten pounds of gold to Edward the goldsmith, asking him to make a beautiful golden pot for his manor home. Edward replies that this may take him several months. Alfred says, "What if I need my gold in the meantime?" "In that case, stop by and get it." Edward gives Alfred a piece of paper saying "The bearer of this bill can come to Edward's goldsmith shop and pick up ten pounds of gold."

Now Alfred is walking around London with a piece of paper whose implicit worth is equal to the market value of ten pounds of gold, minus a risk premium reflecting the possibility that Edward's gold shop might go out of business. This paper can be used in exchange for other goods or as a store of value. It has become money. While merchants who receive the paper have the right, if they wish, to head down to Edward's and get the gold the bill promises, it is easier for them to use the paper again for their next transaction. The buying and selling of goods in the market is thus conducted using pieces of paper, not gold bars.

DEPOSITS ARE MONEY

Another way to think of the situation we've just described is this: Alfred has made a deposit with Edward, and Edward has given him a deposit slip. It's a banking transaction. London's goldsmiths did, in fact, gradually become bankers. Those with wealth in the form of metals left their coins and bars with the goldsmiths, who issued deposit slips that were then used as money. Deposits in banks, in other words, turned stuff money into paper money.

But bank deposits do much more to influence the money supply. London's goldsmiths soon noticed that all of this gold accumulating in their vaults could be turned to profit. Suppose Edward has a storehouse of one thousand gold coins, and on any given day, customers demand only about one hundred of these coins. Most merchants are content to drop off their gold coins and leave them there, conducting almost all of their business with deposit slips. Only rarely does anyone ask to exchange a deposit slip for the gold that backs it up. Edward is overseeing a hoard of unused gold.

What to do with it? Suppose Edward offers to lend the gold to someone, charging interest. Herbert is a reliable merchant who trades between London and Canterbury. Edward lends Herbert 10 gold coins; Herbert uses them to buy five cows; he drives the cows to Canterbury and sells them for 3 gold coins each. The next week Herbert returns with 15 gold coins. He gives Edward his original 10 coins back, plus another for interest. The remaining 4 gold coins are Herbert's profit. Critically, the gold store is again at 1,000 coins; the gold backing the deposit-based paper money is still there in the vault.

What if someone had come in demanding his gold while Herbert was away? Well, Edward has 1,000 coins and has lent out only 10. There are still 990 coins in the vault. On any given day, depositors demand only about 100 coins. It's fairly safe for Edward to lend out 10 coins, because it is very unlikely that *all* of his depositors will come in during the same week and demand *all* of the gold back. If that happened, Edward would be in default of his promises and would be out of business; his bank would fail. But it is very unlikely.

Thus by undertaking a moderate risk, Edward can earn additional profit by lending out gold from his hoard. He can lend more than 10 coins a day, of course. But each additional coin that he lends increases his risk. Were he to lend 1,000 coins a day, he would exhaust his entire store of gold and go into default as soon as even one depositor demanded even 1 gold coin.

When a bank makes loans against its deposits, it accepts a risk of default. The risk depends on how much has been lent versus how much is kept in reserve, as well as the pattern of withdrawals. Edward's risk of failure is minimal so long as he is careful to keep enough gold in the vault to cover any withdrawal requests he is likely to receive. Beyond this, he has some other tools for avoiding failure: he might borrow coins from other banks, or demand coins back from people to whom he has lent them.

For now, however, let's assume that Edward's bank is safe and consider what the practice of lending against deposits means in terms of money. It dramatically increases the amount of money in the economy, and it does so by a process of social reality construction that borders on the magical. After London's bankers developed the practice of deposit-based loans, the world's money became defined far more by collective human psychology than by the actual value of what was exchanged.

Recall that Edward has 1,000 coins in his vault. Because of these deposits, there are effectively 1,000 slips of paper in the economy that say "This slip is worth 1 gold coin in Edward's vault." When Edward lends 10 coins to Herbert, however, the money supply jumps by ten coins. The 1,000 slips of paper worth a gold coin are all still circulating, but now Herbert has 10 more coins. Meanwhile, only 990 coins are actually in the vault. The money supply attributable to Edward the Goldsmith is not 1,000 coins but 1,010, supported by 990 coins of reserves.

Edward created money with his loan. Note that Edward is not the king, declaring something to be money just because he's the king and can lop off the heads of those who disagree. Nor is Edward an alchemist who has turned lead into gold. He is just a goldsmith who lent gold to a trader. Nonetheless, he has increased the amount of money in circulation.

Now suppose that Edward and Herbert tire of conducting their business using gold coins. "Look here," says Herbert, "Why not just give me a paper bill for the coins like you give to everyone else." Instead of handing over gold to Herbert, Edward can issue his loan simply by writing out a new deposit slip that says "The bearer can retrieve 10 gold coins from Edward the Goldsmith." Put another way, Herbert could simply take 10 coins from Edward and then immediately deposit them back into Edward's vault, walking away with a deposit slip instead of coins.

Now we have a gold vault with 1,000 coins backing up a money supply of paper slips valued at 1,010 coins. Edward could make more loans and continue to increase the money supply. The ultimate limit on the amount of money he creates depends on how much risk Edward wants to accept. If he has created 1,000,000 gold coins of paper money against his 1,000 gold coins in reserve, chances are that one day more than 1,000 coins will be demanded from his vault. But by keeping his loans conservative, Edward can create paper money worth several times the value of the hoard in his vault.

The English and broader European banking systems did indeed evolve such lending practices. Long before the era of central banks and monetary policy, what we call "money" thus acquired a strangely unreal—dare we say virtual—character. When 1,000 gold coins support 10,000 paper claims to those coins, it must be the case that several people believe they own the same coin at the same time. Herbert believed the 10 coins in his pocket were his money, since the bank had given them to him; at the same time, Alfred thought they were *his*, since he had deposited them in the first place. Both Alfred and Herbert can use the same 10 gold coins in their trading at the same time. Ten coins magically became 20.

HOW THINGS CAN GO WRONG

When money blossoms from bank deposits, its value rests only on faith. Thus it can go away in the blink of an eye. Suppose Herbert, the borrower, spends his 10 coins to build a new room in his shop. The coins go to George the builder, who walks off with them. Herbert has no money; this is all right because he expects to earn 10 coins of profit in the next few months to be able to pay off his loan on time. But suppose that Edward's bank, on this particular morning, has only 2 gold pieces in the vault. Alfred the depositor comes by to get his 10 coins. Edward the banker confesses that he has only 2 coins, but Alfred demands all 10. Edward, now desperate, calls on Herbert to repay his loan at once. But Herbert has no money with which to pay. The bank has only 2 coins and is obligated to pay 10 to Alfred. It fails.

When Edward's bank fails, some nasty things happen:

- Albert gets 2 coins of the 10 he deposited. The vault is now empty.
- Receivers take over the bank. It is their job to liquidate the failed bank and try to honor as many of its obligations as it can.
- The receivers call on all those to come forward who have a piece of paper saying "The owner of this paper has the right to X coins from Edward's bank."
- The receivers also call on everyone who has borrowed from Edward's bank to repay the loan at once.
- Any funds recovered this way will go to the people who have claims on the bank.

Unfortunately, the bank created far more money through its lending than could be backed by hard coins. Most of the people with paper slips in the name of Edward's bank will therefore go away empty-handed. And as a result, no one will accept these bank notes as money any more. All of that money just disappears—changing from money to mere slips of paper in a blink of an eye.

Then the process cascades. When Edward's bank starts calling in its loans, other institutions are suddenly forced to find money with which to pay. So they start calling in their loans. If they cannot make their payments, they too fail. When one bank fails, the web of trust is broken and the effects ripple outward; each node in the net, breaking, puts stress on all the others, and since the net is tightly stretched under usual circumstances, those others break as well. Understanding this, savvy investors, when they catch the first scent of failure, race immediately to the nearest bank to get their money out before it is too late. Their dash spooks other investors, and eventually we all must race along. It is a bank run; cascading bank runs equal a financial panic.

Nice depictions of bank runs are provided in the popular films *It's a Wonderful Life* and *Mary Poppins*. In real-world financial panics, serious consequences ensue. At several times in the 1800s, panics caused economic activity to contract for years, the unemployment leading to popular revolts. Financial panics in the early 1930s helped bring both Franklin D. Roosevelt and Adolf Hitler to power. The value of money is an important national issue.

STATE MONEY

The value of paper money depends entirely on people's trust in the issuing institution. What if the issuing institution is the state? Governments do not fail the way banks do.

We have seen that, originally, the state, in the form of kings, backed money by minting its own coins. With the advent of paper money economies, state backing evolved into the practice of agreeing to exchange a paper bill for a tangible commodity, typically gold or silver, at a fixed rate. The government then has to make the promise credible by actually maintaining a store of gold and making the exchanges on demand. If successful, this policy establishes a "gold standard" by which any form of money, however flimsy, can be turned into an item of value. The gold standard was the norm for real-world currencies for much of the nineteenth and twentieth centuries. But it did not survive the wars and depressions and price shocks of the past century. The promise to turn slips of paper into gold turned out to be impossible to keep.

Despite the failure of gold and silver standards, the state still officially backs its currency. The state has a monopoly of force. It can take things from people, put them in jail, or even kill them, and no other institution in society can legitimately do that. The state can use this power to make people accept a given object as money. It can declare that if a person refuses to accept seashells as payment for debts, it will levy a fine. Thus the state backs money simply with the force of law. The word "fiat" is used to describe the practice of giving money value by the mere executive decree of the state. Almost all world currencies today are fiat money: they have value because governments say so.

Money, as we have come to know it, is simply backed by the faith and credit of the government. It must be accepted as legal tender—that is, it must be accepted in payment of debts. The U.S. dollar says this right on its face: "This note is legal tender for all debts, public and private." It just is.

DIGITAL MONEY

I would invite you to read that sentence on a dollar in your pocket, but these days, you might not have one. This book is being written in 2013. Money is still issued on paper and in coins, but not exclusively, or even predominantly; most money exists as database entries.

This is where the history of money has gotten us: "real" money, today, is largely nothing more than entries in a digital database backed by the state's promises. I don't know about you, dear reader, but it looks pretty virtual to me.

MONETARY UNIFICATION AND EXPLOSION

Where is this money going? What has humanity discovered about the good and bad features of its formal money systems? For many years, economists agreed that it was best to unify monetary systems. More recently, doubts about unification have arisen. Is it best to have one form of money?

THE CASE FOR A SINGLE CURRENCY

If we go back a millennium or two, monetary affairs were quite simple because not many people were actually involved in a market economy. Typical preindustrial villagers mostly made their own goods and services. If they got something from others, it was usually delivered in the form of a community effort or mutual loans or simply gifts. Villagers didn't need coins.

Neither did preindustrial kings. Kings and nobles in the old world didn't pay for goods and services, they ordered them delivered and done. The lord of the manor was due a certain number of bushels of wheat, a certain number of yards of cloth, a certain number of chickens and pigs each year. Moreover, his stream was to be dredged and his fences repaired. It was simply done and delivered, by ancient agreement. No need for money.

The only people who needed money in this society were merchants and craftsmen, and they were few. Someone whose role was to make barrels all day could not live from eating barrels (although he could wear them and sleep in them). That crafter needed to exchange barrels for other goods, and bartering barrels for those goods on an ongoing basis was tedious. The same can be said for the fellow who buys exotic things from ships, hauls them inland, and sells them to the lords and nobles. It was tedious to haggle over the exchange of pepper against cows.

With so few people actually needing money, the number of different monies in circulation was not a major problem. If you lived in England, you used coin of the English king, but if a coin of Normandy came into your pocket, it would not be too hard to assess its worth in gold and use it for further transactions. At the occasional fair or market, the experts could get together and work out informally what the different coins and monies were worth.

Over most of the world, through most of the history of civilization, money was concentrated in the hands of a few experts. But beginning around A.D. 1100 in Europe, there was a general uptick in economic activity and an expansion in trade. By the time of the Renaissance (A.D. 1400), the number of people whose living involved some kind of trading had increased dramatically. Trading houses existed all across the continent. The number of specialized craftsmen also increased, along with the breadth of items in the typical nobleman's household. Market activity became an ever more important source of the average person's goods and services. Trading that in

A.D. 1200 might have gone on once or twice a year at specialized fairs, by A.D. 1500 occurred daily in the great cities of London, Paris, and Milan. The need for money expanded rapidly.

In A.D. 1200, a French villager might conduct one trade per year, when a merchant came to town. Over his life, he might have market transactions with twelve people, all of them on the village green.[4] Today, a person living in the same French village has direct and indirect market transactions with billions of people all over the world. The toy on his floor was designed in Copenhagen, built in Shanghai, and shipped to France by Americans. While he contemplates this vast web, a Brazilian woman sings a song for him via the internet. The song was recorded by Japanese technicians using materials mined in Zaire. Moreover, many of the goods those people used in their activities are legacy goods, things made months, years, or even decades ago by people who have long since passed away. The Americans work in a 1930s Manhattan skyscraper. The Japanese recording artists like the sound of a vintage 1950s microphone. The paving outside the Frenchman's cottage is three hundred years old.

This vast web of trading emerged only a few centuries ago, and when it did, the need for money expanded vastly. Markets are run by traders in networks. If a network of ten traders needs a certain amount of money to flow freely, how much money does a network of two hundred traders need? The amount grows exponentially with the number of traders.

For four traders, it works out to:

- Trader A: Trades with B, C, and D. That makes three trades.

- Trader B: Trades with C and D. The trade with A is accounted for above. Thus two more trades.
- Trader C: Trades with D. Trades with A and B are already accounted for. Thus one more trade.
- Trader D: All trades accounted for above.

So for four traders, the number of trades per day is six. In a formula, the number of trades among N traders is

$$\text{Number of trades} = (N{-}1) + (N{-}2) + (N{-}3) + \ldots + (N{-}(N{-}1))$$

With some manipulation, it can be shown that this equals:

$$\text{Number of trades} = \tfrac{1}{2}\,(N^2{-}N)$$

This formula reveals a basic property of networks: when the number of nodes (traders) grows, the number of connections grows by the square. Our four-trader network conducted 6 trades per day. A ten-trader network conducts 45. This seems manageable. But a network of 200 traders conducts 19,900 trades per day, and 10,000 traders conduct almost 50 million. Money is needed for each trade. Thus as an economy goes from precommercial to commercial, its demand for money rises very rapidly.

Think how costly it is to haggle in such an environment.[5] It is one thing when the system must bear one hundred or two hundred haggling moments a day, quite another when there are fifty million. Suppose, in the preceding examples, that one of every ten trades requires haggling about the worth of something.

Here's the relationship of trader network to haggles per trader per day:

Traders	Haggles per trader per day
4	0.3
10	0.9
200	19.9
10,000	999.9

No trader can manage to haggle a thousand times a day. Therefore, keeping the haggling rate down is obviously important to smooth functioning of the entire system, and its importance grows exponentially with the size of the commercial economy.

This is why the people who manage economies begin to pay attention to what seem like tiny details. What size should the coins be? Should the sales tax be raised by a tenth of a point? Should we use slips of paper to record trades? For any one person, such changes mean nothing. But across an entire system, the trading efficiency gained or lost can be immense.

Multiple currencies provide an example of how important trading efficiencies can become. When commerce flourished in early modern Europe, it did so in an environment where at first there were hundreds of currencies. Here are a few of the major ones:

- Heller
- Kreuzer
- Pfennig
- Gulden

- Taler
- Ducat
- Florin
- Grot
- Groschen
- Shilling
- Pound
- Guinea
- Denier
- Sol
- Livre
- Soldo
- Lira
- Kopek
- Ruble
- Real
- Besant
- Dinar[6]

And these are just the major *categories* of money. For each type, different states might offer their own versions. There were florins of Liege and florins of Genoa, ducats of Naples and ducats of Hungary. As the early modern period progressed, those working in the commercial economy began to understand that things would go better with fewer currencies. As the nation-state evolved, one of the scale efficiencies it captured was to enact currency conformity across wider and wider regions. A France made up of many dukedoms, abbacies, and principalities had to deal with a surfeit of coinage types. As the French royal house came to control more and more of the French landscape, its preferred coin came to dominate an ever larger economic realm, and the number of competing currencies fell. French traders began to enjoy efficiencies that traders in Germany and Italy could only dream of.

How do we know that currency was critical to the development of nation-states? The example of Germany, lacking unified currency, is illustrative. After the Peace of Westphalia in 1648, some regions of Europe emerged nationally and culturally coherent under a unified governing structure, and some did not. France, England, and Sweden fell into the former category: ruling and ruled situated together, in a region with a broadly shared linguistic and cultural history. Germany and Italy, meanwhile, were mixtures of independent small states and small regions ruled by noble houses with widely spread holdings. And to each ruler his currency.[7]

Germans eventually became resentful of their lack of national unity, and with the nineteenth century came much political striving to unify the country. When the country was unified under Otto von Bismarck in 1871, one of his first acts of state was to implement a unified currency. This had been anticipated thirty-five years earlier by an attempt to unify the country economically. Members of various German states came together in the 1820s and 1830s to remove tolls and taxes on trade between them. In 1837 they concluded a treaty of currency that set the Vereinstaler (the union dollar) as the standard against which other currencies could be measured. Currency unification and standardization was seen as a necessary first step in making a country. When the two Germanies separated by World War II first discussed reunification in 1989–1990, the first proposal was for an "economic and currency union." Political unification only came later.

A unified currency was seen as so advantageous that in the twentieth century many efforts were made around the world to systematize and reduce currency clutter. The old royal and noble coinages died away. More and more commerce was conducted in terms of a few supercurrencies. Efforts were made to peg those currencies to some standard, such as gold. If that had been successful, the currencies could also have been pegged to one another at a fixed value. But a system of international fixed currency exchange rates proved impossible to sustain, as each economy had its own unique needs for higher or lower money growth rates.

Thus was born the idea of a unified European currency. It would not be tied to any fixed commodity, but it would be centrally administered by the European states. The result is the euro, which, whatever its troubles, embodies a centuries-long struggle to reduce the drag of haggling on trade.

At first the euro was a purely virtual currency. It was launched in 1999 as digital assets in bank accounts. The first notes were not printed until 2002. For three years, the euro was play money, like a game's gold pieces. Today, it represents the most advanced effort in history to unify money across political domains.

The history of currency unification reminds us then that there are strong economic incentives to reduce monetary confusion. It seems ideal to have just one form of money, so that everyone knows how to speak about the value of things. Money is like a language—the entire system runs faster when we all speak the same language.

THE CASE FOR MANY CURRENCIES

While a single currency is more efficient for transactions, it prevents economic managers from tailoring the institutions of money to local circumstances. Economic well-being depends on the growth rate of money and the ways it is created, awarded, and traded. A monetary policy may suit the needs of most regions in an area but be harmful for a few. Economist Martin Feldstein predicted that the single European currency would be a problem because of the very different development status of Europe's regions.[8] Suppose that when Portugal needs monetary growth, Germany needs stability and low inflation. Germany, being bigger, wins the debate. Portugal, unable to boost its economy, suffers unemployment and contraction. The struggles of the euro indicate that a single currency is not in fact the inevitable endpoint of the evolution of money. The multiple monies of humanity's past were not necessarily foolish. Efficiency of exchange is not everything; money serves many other purposes.

Perhaps money is not a technical gadget with a single best way of fitting to the social machine. David Wolman argues that "the whole idea of a global currency was planted in our heads by leftist utopians and science fiction authors."[9] If it is good to have many currencies, how many? Should the United States have a different official currency for each state in the Union? Why not for every county?

To summarize this lengthy discussion, it is apparent that there has been an evolution away from concrete, tangible forms of money toward paper money. Along the way, money became tangled up in the banking system. This has created a management issue: sustaining confidence in the value of money requires keeping banks healthy.

The state has stepped in to back the money, first by offering exchanges of paper against metals, then by simply declaring that the money is the money. Finally, the state has pursued unification of money in order to reduce economic inefficiency, but this policy is now under fire.

COMPANY MONEY

Today, money generally involves banks and the state. Yet virtual currencies are issued by companies that are not banks. Where did company money come from?

The institutions of corporate-issued money have emerged in two forms. The first form is commercial paper. Earlier I explained how goldsmiths, who were private citizens, issued paper deposit slips that were used for money. In fact, private companies of all kinds also issued such slips. For example, suppose that Frank's Restaurant buys $10,000 in tables from Jane's Furniture. Frank now owes Jane $10,000. Jane therefore prints up a bill that states, "Frank's Restaurant owes me $10,000." Jane can now use this piece of paper to pay her own debts. Say she buys a boat. She tells the boat seller, "Take this paper down to Frank's Restaurant and he will give you the money." The bill acts like paper money. It functions just fine, so long as all the businesses trust one another's promises.

Over time, instruments like Jane's bill evolved into direct promises by companies to make payments. These promises are called "commercial paper." A large company that needs to meet a $10 million payroll today might sell ten pieces of paper for $1 million each; the paper says, "This company will pay the bearer $1.01 million in 3 months." The company gets its cash today, and the investor gets a promise of profit (because $1.01 million is more than $1 million). During those three months, the piece of paper can be used in all kinds of transactions and represents a form of currency very similar to paper money—except that it is issued by a private company.[10]

Company money has emerged from another source, however. In the late nineteenth century, two different retail entities had the idea of issuing a private currency on a large scale at roughly the same time. In 1888, Coca-Cola began sending out paper tickets that enabled the bearer to receive a free Coke from a local vendor. It was a marketing move—the paper tickets were a shrewd way to put the product in the buyer's eye and a way to lower the costs of trying the product. The tickets worked for the retailers because Coca-Cola compensated them. The underlying marketing strategy is simple but effective: if nobody knows about your product and trying it out is critical to success, then you should lower the price of first use as much as possible. Whatever you lose by giving away free product, you gain back by widening the product's market. By the early twentieth century, Coke had become a household word, and other companies, notably the Post cereal company, began offering free product or reduced rates to the bearers of paper documents, by then called "coupons."

In 1896, the Sperry and Hutchison company began offering "S&H Green Stamps" to retailers. Green Stamps are different from Coke's tickets. Retailers bought the stamps and could choose when, where, and how to distribute them to customers. On receiving the stamps, customers could collect them. Each stamp had a face value in points. S&H then issued a catalog of products that could be "redeemed" for stamp points. The purpose was not so much to introduce a product to new customers, as with Coke's coupons, but to retain the customers one had. While it is true that a company could try to accomplish this by simply lowering its prices, the stamps seemed to have a loyalty effect beyond what could be attained by lowering prices. There is an experiential effect—call it entertainment—in receiving a handful of stamps, carefully licking them and placing them in a booklet, then using the booklets to buy things from a special catalog. S&H became a large and profitable company.

Today, customer loyalty programs are everywhere. Sometimes it's just a card that you get stamped for every cup of coffee you buy— turn in a filled card for a free cup! More often it's a digital database-driven rewards program, which, by now, everyone has. It is difficult to make any face-to-face retail purchase today without being asked whether you have your company loyalty card or account number. When you produce your card, some sort of points or credits are added to it, and eventually those points are redeemable for goods, services, or discounts. Or you pay a regular fee to have the card, and it can then be used to lower the prices you pay.

Frequent flyer miles (FFM) are perhaps the leading example of points systems. They date to the 1980s, when deregulation forced airlines to become more concerned about customer loyalty. FFMs work on a simple idea: the more you fly, the more miles you get on your account. Miles can then be redeemed for future flights. The system is clearly modeled after the cup-of-coffee system, but the connection between miles in your account and the miles you actually fly is sketchy. Most airlines offer a minimum number of miles per segment flown; if I fly one hundred miles from Bloomington to

Indianapolis, I still get five hundred FFM credits. And the airlines offer FFMs for all kinds of other activities, like signing up for a credit card. FFMs are usually spent buying flights, but they can also be used for things like seating upgrades. You can even sell your FFMs; the website cashyourmiles.com offers (at the time of writing) between 1 and 1.4 U.S. cents per mile.[11] On the whole, the FFM is simply a currency that is mostly earned by flying on the airline's planes.

The growing use of company points as money is somewhat startling. Consider Amazon.com. At Amazon, anyone can sell almost anything, by signing up as a nonprofessional seller. Searching just now I find, in addition to the usual books and music, a 29dB gain hearing aid for $34.95; an InterDesign 255 00 Clean and Dirty Dishwasher Indicator for $4.73; and a gas-powered thirty-three-ton log splitter for $2,299.99. Amazon accepts reward points from numerous credit cards, including its own. It also has Amazon Coin, which for now can only be used for eBooks. But it could be used, in principle, for anything on Amazon. Thus we already have a system where "points" and "coins" can buy almost anything. The one thing that keeps these virtual monies from being a currency is that they are not directly transferable to other people. I cannot give you my Amazon Coins or my Amazon Rewards points. On the other hand, buying things on Amazon for other people is seamless: you simply ship it to their house instead of yours. I can use my points to buy you things. I can also turn my points and coins into dollars by selling you the login information to my account. There is no evidence that anyone has done this yet, although the practice of selling an account is quite common in online games. The purchasing power can indeed be moved around. The combination of company points and product offerings makes Amazon effectively an emerging alternative economy.

Coupons and stamps and frequent flyer miles and rewards points and Facebook Credits—are they money? Are they virtual money? While I will address this more closely in Chapter 4, company points do seem to have many features of money. You can (and do) see the value of all kinds of goods expressed in terms of the stamps, coupons, and company points needed to get them. Moreover, the points and coupons and FFMs can be held for a long time and they retain their purchasing power. The vast majority of FFMs sit in accounts unused.

But one important function of money that company points do not serve particularly well is as a medium of exchange. There is usually only one channel for exchange: the points or whatever are given to a single company in return for a limited range of goods. You cannot give the company other things of value (such as dollars) to obtain the points. A customer could not buy Green Stamps from S&H directly; she had to get them by shopping at an affiliated retailer.

Similarly, people do not generally exchange stamps, coupons, or points with one another. In principle, we could. I could go to Target with you and let you use my Target card to buy a lime green polo shirt or a brown-and-pink pencil holder. You could buy me a flight with your Jet Blue miles. The companies erect walls to discourage these behaviors because the point, historically, has been to cement the relationship between the buyer and the seller.

All this seems to be changing. Increasingly, the main use of a company currency is not to retain loyalty but to acquire and then sell data about the customer's behavior. Everyone enrolled in a company loyalty program has all of his or her purchases recorded in the company's databases, where they can be cross-referenced against the customer's personal data—sex, address, age, occupation. Databases are valuable.

The informational motivation for company money creates a different set of incentives. If I enroll you in CastronovaPoints primarily to sell your behavioral data to others, then I want to get as much data as I possibly can. If you want to use your CPs to buy things other than lectures about games, technology, and society, that's OK with me! I am happy to contract with the local gas station to accept CPs as payment, because if my data includes what kind of gas you buy, it will be more valuable to the people to whom I'm selling it. There's no limit at all—the most valuable data set is the one that contains every recordable moment you have ever experienced. Every company's data program—not *loyalty* program, but *data* program—wants to grow. So we see credit card rewards programs that allow you to spend your reward points on everything from cruises to hats. These systems still do not allow you to transfer rewards to other people, but it is hard to see why they would not. Information about who gives what gifts to whom is extremely valuable. There is already a nascent, awkward system for gifting company points, through the purchase of gift cards both tangible and digital. These are almost always denominated in real-world currency. It would be simple for a company to allow users to transfer their points at will. Perhaps the hesitancy is that this would sever any tie between the points in someone's account and her loyalty to the issuing company. One could imagine a drug dealer, for example, with a massive accumulation of Target rewards without ever having bought anything there with real money.

Recent innovations in company money suggest that this is a place where the line between real money and virtual money may evaporate completely. Consider the debit card. It began in the 1960s and 1970s with teller cards, which allowed people to retrieve money from cash machines any time, day or night. That gave you access around the clock to funds stored only in digital form in your bank account. You went to the machine, got the money, and went to the grocery store. Debit cards removed the physical cash from this process. With a debit card, the funds go directly from your bank to the grocer. This makes the currency completely virtual.

A similar development happens through PayPal, a payments service owned by the online auction giant eBay. More than 100 million people worldwide have active PayPal accounts. When you sign up, you enter payment information of your choice (typically a bank account number or a credit card). You can then use PayPal to buy things on the internet. You can even send someone money using email. It also works the other way—once PayPal has your bank account information, it can forward money that people send you into your account. PayPal also allows you to store balances within its system.

There is evidence that company money and game virtual monies are growing together. The game company Zynga recently partnered with American Express to launch a prepaid debit card that offers in-game rewards. Use the card to buy real bananas, and you earn points toward virtual bananas. A virtual currency exchange service called FirstMeta claims that it will be able, on launch, to transfer value among multiple virtual currencies and multiple real currencies as well.[12]

All of this activity indirectly turns real currency into virtual currency. Online systems allow people to transfer dollar, euro, and yen values among one another without a physical medium. We have already entered the era in which all "real" currencies are virtual. The differences among Amazon points and gold pieces and the euro lie not in their tangibility but in their legal status, functions, and customs of use. Even though company monies were initially launched to serve limited ends of customer loyalty and marketing, in the information age they too are expanding to become a new type of currency.

CRAFT MONEY

As money has become more flexible, private actors have invented new kinds in pursuit of private goals. Bitcoin could be viewed primarily as a craft money; its inventors apparently are motivated only by the desire to provide the world with a form of money that offers benefits other forms do not. Other examples include fair-CASH, which aims to protect consumer privacy, and "community currencies" whose purpose is to protect local markets from unwanted connection to the global economy. The community currency movement even has its own research journal.[13]

PLAY MONEY

We have seen the emergence of money in general, then state money, then company money, then craft money. Many of the virtual currencies we see today, however, emerged from none of these sources directly. Many new currency creation and management systems were invented and developed in online games; that's where the know-how emerged that allows private concerns to manage private economies with millions of users. Thirty years ago, if you cracked open a book and saw on the first page an argument that business and policy experts should look into the monies being used in video games, you would, if you had any sense, have simply put the book down again. Yet here we are. A normal person observing the explosion of wildcat currencies is right to ask, where did anyone get the idea to create a purely digital currency and use it for exchange within a closed system? The answer is, "in online games."[14]

GODS

According to Richard Bartle, who coinvented the first online multiplayer game in 1978, the first online game to use its own currency was Gods. At that time, an online game was simply a set of command entries followed by computer responses. You used a terminal program to log into a computer. Once logged in, you had a screen with some text, and a command line. You entered commands and the computer would send more informational sentences to the screen. A multiplayer game in this format might say "Fred has entered the game." At that point you could type, "say Hi Fred" and hit enter. The text "You say Hi Fred" would appear. On Fred's computer, the text "{your name} says Hi Fred" would appear. If you typed "go n," the computer might respond, "You go North. You are now standing on the Moors of Doom. There is a goblin here!" You would have to type "attack" or "run" or "say Hi Fred" and see what happened. Maybe the Goblin was named Fred, too.

This mode of gaming is the text-based MUD, for "multiuser dungeon." Coins were used from the very beginning, but only as a means of buying goods from the system. Gods was apparently the first one to allow people to buy and sell things with one another. That was in 1985.

GEMSTONE III

Gemstone is a text-based MUD that was introduced in 1987. It still exists, as of this writing, in the form of Gemstone IV, published by Simutronics. The game made its greatest contribution to this story in the early 1990s, when its economy became one of the first used by outsiders to make money. Virtual money was an important route to advancement, and Gemstone allowed players to gift the in-world currency to one another. A flourishing out-world trade emerged, in which those who had accumulated balances in the game sold them for real money, either to those starting out or those who, for whatever reason, wanted more in-game wealth. In the early 2000s I spoke with a gamer who claimed to "own" the entire Gemstone economy and to be managing it "for" the developers. The game had some 2,000–2,500 consistent players, so this was like running the economy of a small town. The man's only claim to this power was in the fact that most of the money spent in Gemstone went through his hands at some point. The gold sellers sold to him, and he in turn sold the gold they had collected to other players.

What at the time seemed a bizarre episode in a small text-based online game soon proved to be the harbinger of a much larger issue. The question was—is this fair? To some it might look like cheating to use outside money to gain an advantage in a game. In the United

States and Europe, this trading of real money for gold pieces, or RMT (real-money trade), as it came to be known, was treated as a problem. It certainly disrupted the game's economic design, which was based on the idea that money would enter the system as fast as normal players would generate it in their adventuring. The economy was not designed with gold farming in mind—that is, with hordes of people who were not actually playing the game coming in solely to kill monsters and take their loot for sale to genuine players. This activity completely violated the fantasy parameters of the space. When people play a fantasy game, the argument goes, their enjoyment depends on its being a fantasy. Having someone appear suddenly with immense powers and wealth simply because he spent thousands of dollars on game money and gear wrecks the game experience for others.

The legal status of game currencies was thrown into doubt. Was it legal, in the game's terms, to sell game money to other players? In the board game Monopoly, for example, it is certainly not within the rules to pull out a twenty and offer to buy Boardwalk from another player. Some online games banned the practice; others welcomed it. Still others stated that RMT was illegal but did nothing about it.

Then there was the real-world legality of the practice. An online game requires users to accept a lengthy terms-of-service agreement and end user–licensing agreement before they can play. Often these agreements forbid a player from selling currency or other game items to other players. Is that a fair contract?[15]

LINEAGE

Lineage, launched in 1997, was the first large-scale immersive 3D online game. It created a genre: the MMORPG, or massively multiplayer online roleplaying game. "Massive" was apt: the game quickly had more than a million players. It also legitimized the buying and selling of game currency in ways no previous game had done. Lineage was a Korean game, and in Korean culture it was considered within the parameters of normal game play to spend real money to buy game money and thus gain an in-game advantage. The Korean online game industry proceeded with the understanding that players not only would engage in RMT but would do so without scruple. For Korean game companies, the question was not "What's our stance on RMT and how do we stop it if we want to?" but "How do we make money from our players' evident desire to spend real money on game items?"

For ten years after the launch of Lineage, the standard revenue model for online game play was the monthly subscription. Typically $15 per month, the subscription gave the player access to everything in the game. But the emergence of a huge side industry in selling game currency led to a different model, the free-to-play, or freemium, model. You could play with no subscription fee, but your access to game content was restricted. Free accounts could do only so much. To get access to special items, areas, and powers, a player had to move to a monthly subscription or, more often, make a one-time payment to unlock the content. Companies also began to offer smaller items for sale in small amounts, in what was known as the microtransaction model. Currencies were used to make this kind of market liquid. Individual items of armor might be sold directly to the user, but what if the armor had some tiny real-world value? Selling it to the user at pennies per piece would not make sense, as transaction costs would eat up the revenue. Instead, players were allowed to buy lots of five hundred or five thousand crowns for $5 or $10, and the game money would then be used to buy the armor. The balance could be spent on other things. This led eventually to a dual-currency model now so prominent in virtual economies: one currency can be obtained only through game play; the other can be bought with dollars.

This evolution in the game space was, in effect, a takeover by the game companies of the lucrative business of selling game currency. It makes sense—if RMT is a valuable service, why let third parties benefit from it? Why not bring it in house?

SECOND LIFE

There was a critical U.S.-based innovator along these lines, though not in the game space. Second Life is a platform, not a game, and the service it has provided allows users to create virtual spaces on virtual land. In its early years, SL offered its owners, Linden Labs, a unique revenue model. Simply put, SL was a landowner that sold parcels for money. It also issued a currency, the Linden Dollar, that users could trade with one another. SL evolved a vast economy as users made various digital objects and then sold them. Legitimate amounts of real money were made in Second Life land speculation. Linden Labs allowed its dollar to trade freely against the U.S. dollar, and its value held steady. Moreover, the company broke new ground in openly publishing its economic data, a practice followed by only a few other companies (notably CCP, makers of EVE Online). SL made an important point, that virtual economies and virtual currencies had value for a business that was focused not on games but on self-representation services and social networks.

MAGIC THE GATHERING AND DUNGEON KILL POINTS

In all of these cases, the play money was backed and managed by individual companies. There are important examples, however, of games in which a money emerged without any action by the company. Magic the Gathering was, as we have seen, at first a purely physical game: players with physical decks of cards competing face to face. Yet when MtG went online it spawned a virtual currency, the Event Ticket. The currency emerged because there was a need for currency and an object that could serve as currency.

This is not an isolated phenomenon and has in fact become generalized in the form of dragon kill points, or DKP.[16] DKP emerged to answer a need among the community of raiding gamers. Raiding is a gaming practice in which large groups of players, sometimes hundreds, will go together into a dungeon to take on a particularly nasty monster that the designers have placed there for exactly this purpose. In many games, these monsters offer the very best loot. They also offer their loot rarely, representing a very high challenge-reward pairing. That is, not only is the monster so tough that you have to coordinate with dozens or hundreds of other real people to kill him, he also has limited amounts of treasure. To compensate, and keep it worthwhile, the designers make the monster's loot extremely powerful—"the best axe in the game" and so forth.

This creates a problem for an axe-wielding adventurer. How many times do I have to go on this adventure before I get my axe? I teamed up with 199 people on March 17, we killed the monster, and he surrendered a powerful wand. That was great for the wizard on our team, but worthless for an axe bearer. The next time, April 12, it was a bow. Great for hunters; not me. On May 22, armor of stealth—great for thieves, but I am not a thief.

Finally, on June 1, my time came! He dropped the rebounding axe of utter destruction! Hurray! Unfortunately, among the 200 raiders that day, there were 10 axemen. We rolled randomly to see who would get the axe, and of course I didn't get it. What's worse, this is my fourth raid, helping other people, and the guy who got the axe was on his first raid. That seems unfair. How many times do I have to go on this adventure before I get my axe?

DKP systems emerged to solve this problem. A leader, whose office is not formally assigned by the game company but simply emerges among the players, assigns dragon kill points to every player who participates in a raid. The leader is usually an officer of a player "guild" or club. The club maintains a website and a database in which it records its members' DKP. Every time our axeman goes on a raid, he gets a few more DKP. And then when the rebounding axe of utter destruction is found, all the axemen use their DKP to bid for the item. When one player wins the axe, the officer records the high bid and subtracts it from the winning player's DKP account.

DKP is thus a currency used to allocate scarce, rare goods to players based on their commitment to raiding. The currency is issued by players, recorded by players, and redeemed by players. It is freely transferable, or can be made so depending on the policies of the guild.

DKP has grown as an institution as the practice of raiding has evolved. At one time, almost all raiding was done by small groups of elite players in tightly knit guild clans, where they all knew one another well in real life. Game practice and design has gradually made raiding available to more average, casual players. As this has occurred, the use of DKP to allocate raid goods has widened as well. There are off-the-shelf programs that implement a DKP system for guild officers who are too busy to create and manage one on their own. For example, the program eqDKP in the game World of Warcraft automatically interfaces with the game's servers and records data on which players attended which raids. It displays the amounts to players and allows them to bid on loot.

These graphical DKP programs amount to automated software that allows just about anybody to issue and manage his or her own virtual currency, for any purpose whatsoever. At the start of the twenty-first century, as at the start of the sixteenth, the lines between commodity, personal item, and official currency are becoming very, very blurred.

3

IS IT LEGAL?

Is it legal for private actors to issue their own currency?

The answer will differ by jurisdiction, of course, but for convenience, let's focus on the United States. Therefore:

Is it legal in the United States for private actors to issue their own currency?

Don't bother looking in the U.S. Constitution for the answer. The Framers neglected to mention the World of Warcraft Gold Piece or the Amazon Coin. You might be surprised to learn that they didn't define the dollar either. The Constitution gives Congress the power to coin money and regulate its value. It does not say what the coin is, although it mentions "dollars" in a couple of places. But the Constitution nowhere forbids those outside the government to coin their own money.[1] Nonetheless, U.S. citizen Bernard von NotHaus was sent to jail recently for, as the U.S. attorney said, "minting his own currency."[2] Was the Justice Department right? Is there a law against private money? The rules about money, in the United States at least, are not in the nation's founding documents but have emerged over the decades.

HOW THE DOLLAR BECAME THE DOLLAR

It wasn't until the Second Congress that that body got around to defining the nation's money. The dollar was established in 1792 as a coin with 371¼ grains of pure silver. It was heavy metal money. The penalty for debasing the currency was death, a provision that remains in effect today, even though the government mints few gold or silver coins.

While the dollar was defined in terms of commodities, not all money was issued in commodity form. The government issued paper money, "backed" by silver and gold in its vaults. The paper gave the bearer the right to exchange the paper for real silver and gold at fixed amounts. As we saw in the previous chapter, anyone sitting on a hoard of gold and silver can issue many times the amount of the hoard in the form of paper bills and be relatively safe from failure. From one hundred gold bars in the vault, a government can issue one thousand or more slips of paper saying, "This can be exchanged for a gold bar in the government vault." Provided no more than one hundred holders of the paper actually demand their gold bars at any one time, the government can sustain quite a bit more money in the system than it has in its vaults.

The United States issued money this way until the Civil War, when the pressures of the conflict required Washington to print (and spend) so much paper money that it began to have difficulty meeting paper holders' requests to exchange their bills for gold and silver. In the crisis, Congress made the step to fiat money—passing legislation allowing the government to print $150 million in paper money and requiring that actors in the economy accept it as legal tender.[3] In 1870 the Supreme Court had to rule on the validity of this action. In its description of the case, the Court put the word "dollar" in quotation marks. It distinguished between two aspects of money. On one hand, you can issue money. On the other, you can require people to accept as legal tender a "money" already in existence. There seemed to be no doubt that the government can issue currency in whatever form it wishes, whether metal disks or beaver pelts. Yet Chief Justice Chase wrote:

> We are not aware that it has ever been claimed that the power to issue bills or notes has any identity with the power to make them a legal tender. On the contrary, the whole history of the country refutes that notion. The states have always been held to possess the power to authorize and regulate the issue of bills for circulation by banks or individuals, subject, as has been lately determined, to the control of Congress, for the purpose of establishing and securing a national currency; and yet the states are expressly prohibited by the Constitution from making anything but gold and silver coin a legal tender. This seems decisive on the point that the power to issue notes and the power to make them a legal tender are not the same power, and that they have no necessary connection with each other.[4]

There are several things to note about this. First, the court is entirely blasé about the fact that, while the government had been issuing currency, so had private banks and even individuals. These banks and individuals had come under regulation, but there was apparently no sense that their issuing currency might be illegal. By 1870, private individuals and banks in advanced economies had been doing this for several centuries at least. It was an established practice.

Second, the Court ruled that issuing money and enforcing acceptance of it are completely different questions, and it finds no trace of any power for the latter in the Constitution or precedent. Thus the Court ruled that no one could be forced to accept a currency, even one issued by the national government, as money.

This precedent did not last. A powerful counterargument, that the government's emergency powers must include the ability to issue paper and make it legal tender, carried the Court within a few years. By the end of the nineteenth century, the Court had clearly proclaimed the government's power to issue fiat money. Despite this, the United States continued to make its paper money convertible to gold and silver. Though it had the power to issue paper at will, it hesitated to do so.

In 1933, the financial crises induced by the Great Depression led to extraordinary monetary policy.[5] President Roosevelt issued an executive order requiring all U.S. citizens and private concerns to deliver their gold to the Federal Reserve and receive $20.67 per ounce in paper money. With no private gold in the economy, the state's money had one fewer currency to compete with. At that time, contracts could have clauses requiring payment in the form of gold.

Once Roosevelt's executive order put all the legally sanctioned gold in government vaults, Congress voided these gold clauses, effectively removing gold as a means of payment. These moves were reaffirmed in the Gold Reserve Act of 1934 and subsequently approved by the Supreme Court.

The U.S. government (like other governments around the world) continued to exchange paper bills for gold and silver for several decades, primarily as part of its trade with other countries. Even this broke down in the 1970s. Today, almost all modern economies are based on fiat money, whose purchasing power comes only from the general faith that the money has purchasing power.[6] State-backed fiat money remained the only general currency until the recent explosion of virtual money.[7]

THE LEGAL STATUS OF PRIVATE MONEY

The issuing of private paper money by banks and other private individuals is an old practice. In nineteenth-century America there were two interesting restrictions on this activity.[8] First, the governments of individual U.S. states could not *issue* money—the Constitution reserved this right for the central government. Second, however, individual states could *regulate* the issuing of money by private banks headquartered in their jurisdictions. Several states, for instance, permitted banks to issue money only in large denominations. This was done to force banks to retain adequate gold reserves. The theory was that holders of large denomination bills were more likely to return to the bank and exchange those bills for gold. As a result, banks would have to keep more gold on hand. A bank with more reserves is less likely to fail. The states hoped to make the financial system more secure.

These restrictions on small denominations led to a strange situation: the money was too big! Imagine if today the only money we had was $100 bills. How would you buy a soft drink? Under these circumstances, in the mid-1800s, American farmers and merchants issued their own money.[9] Some of this money had "dollars" printed on it; other bills were denominated in goods and services. A farmer's note, for instance, might say, "Good for ten bushels of wheat from Farmer Brown." In 1851, the government responded to the big-money problem by issuing a three-penny coin, the trime.[10] But private individuals' legal power to issue money was not questioned.

This changed in the Civil War. First, in order to secure the purchasing power of its own smaller notes, the government forbade the issuing of private money in denominations smaller than $1. A dollar then was worth more than it is today: a pound of bacon cost six cents. Private individuals could still issue money denominated in goods and services. But in 1864, Congress outlawed issuing any metal coinage intended for use as money. These restrictions largely drove private money out of the economy.

Nonetheless, the banking crises of the 1930s brought the return of local private currencies. As banks had difficulty making their payments, or failed altogether, people responded by hoarding their money, fearing to put it in the hands of others because they might never see it again. This hurt the banks even more and also created a currency shortage—there was no money to pay for things. Companies resorted to paying their employees in private money, called "scrip," which was dollar-denominated and carried the promise to be redeemable in "real" money. This "real" money, ironically, was the U.S. dollar, which had grown so scarce as to be almost completely unreal.

The issuing of scrip was allowed because the scrip was local money, not intended for general circulation. It was limited in time, place, and terms of exchange. Whether or not these are reasonable bounds for private money, such bounds have not been placed in current law.

Federal law today is vague on the status of private money. Title 18, chapter 17, section 336 of the U.S. Code forbids anyone to issue money worth less than $1. Chapter 25, section 486 forbids making a metal coin for general currency—violation punishable by five years' imprisonment. Section 491 similarly punishes anyone who makes, issues, or passes any coin, card, token, or device in metal or its compounds, intended to be used as money. It goes on to forbid the counterfeiting of any token, disk, paper, or other device "issued or authorized in connection with rationing of food or fiber distribution by any agency of the United States."

These laws were the basis for the prosecution of Mr. von NotHaus, who issued "Liberty Dollars" that generally looked and felt like U.S. dollar coins. The U.S. attorney's press release on the case is headlined "Defendant Convicted of Minting His Own Currency," although the actual charges in the case were "making coins resembling and similar to United States coins; issuing, passing, selling, and possessing Liberty Dollar coins; issuing and passing Liberty Dollar coins intended for use as current money; and conspiracy against the United States."[11] If we read this carefully, it seems that Mr. von NotHaus was convicted for making money that was similar to U.S. money—not for making private money per se.

Nonetheless, it appears that the U.S. government believes that it has the power to regulate any and all private money. During legal proceedings in the von NotHaus case, the federal prosecutor claimed that the government has a broad power to restrain the circulation of private money. The judge in the case did not agree that this claim was necessary to the case and struck this language in his ruling. His actions left the government's claim undecided.

So: is it legal in the United States for private actors to issue their own currency? No one knows.

THE LEGAL STATUS OF REWARDS PROGRAMS

Most of the law regarding rewards programs centers around their taxability, not their status as currency. Though discussions go back thirty years, the taxability of frequent flyer miles is still unresolved.[12] Since 2002, the U.S. Internal Revenue Service has not pursued enforcement of taxes on promotional benefits.[13] But in March 2012, Citibank, which had for years given FFMs to customers who opened new accounts, decided to issue tax forms to these new account holders that reported the FFMs as income.[14] The account holders filed a class-action lawsuit. Thus while the IRS views reward points as price reductions or rebates, at least one major company fears they may be income.

But consider the following case from Canada. In 2007, Clark Johnson traveled from Thunder Bay, Ontario, to Chicago for medical treatment. To do so, he cashed in frequent flyer miles in the Air Canada Aeroplan system and also paid $220 out of pocket. At tax time, he claimed the $220 as a medical expense. The Canada Revenue

Agency accepted this. But Johnson also claimed the value of the Aeroplan points he used as a medical expense as well. He argued that if purchased entirely out of pocket, the flight would have cost $2,280. The seventy-six thousand miles he used thus had a value of three cents per mile. It was also possible to buy FFMs directly from Aeroplan at three cents per mile. The CRA agreed that there had been a transfer of "money's worth" from Johnson to Aeroplan, but that since no Canadian money left his pocket, he had not actually paid anything. In 2010, the judge in the case ruled that the phrase "amount paid" can also include the transfer of a right, such as the right to cash in FFMs for flights.[15] This ruling effectively turned FFMs into money and perhaps explains why, two years later, a large American bank decided to report its issuing of FFMs as money as well.

None of this suggests that reward points are illegal. West's Encyclopedia of American Law describes trading stamps and coupons (a category in which it includes FFMs) as tokens of legal obligations. They represent a promise to provide something of value. Thus they involve contractual law as well as criminal law, since the production of a "redeemable" token that cannot be redeemed is a form of fraud.

To the question, Are Frequent Flyer Miles money under the law, and are they permitted, we can conclusively answer, "Perhaps."

THE LEGAL STATUS OF VIRTUAL PROPERTY

Let's now consider virtual money, gold pieces and credits that have never had and never will have any tangible manifestation. We could try to fit them into the law of rewards programs, but as we have seen, that would not tell us much.

Several legal scholars have recently addressed the legal status of virtual property. In a groundbreaking analysis, Greg Lastowka and Dan Hunter argued that virtual items have to be considered property under the general historical and legal understanding of that word.[16] There seems to be little difference between a URL or web address and a virtual gold piece.[17] Both are intangible goods over which someone has claimed ownership, even if they do not fit well in existing classes of intangibles such as intellectual property. Since the courts and Congress have long since recognized a property right in URLs, Lastowka and Hunter wrote, they should recognize property rights in virtual goods. But in a later paper, Lastowka offers a counterargument: unlike a URL, the property created by games and social media developers is only artificially scarce.[18] Virtual goods seem to be like acreage, chairs, and hairpieces only because the designers have made them so. They are not inherently property but only constructed into property. Lastowka answers this argument by noting that many valuable things are designed to have only artificial scarcity. His examples are high fashion and baseball cards, but he could as easily have mentioned the U.S. dollar. It too is intangible and has value only through the management of its scarcity. If dollars and baseball cards are property, how can a virtual helmet or gold piece not be?

The law has not really taken up this matter. The few U.S. court decisions that might touch on the status of virtual property have instead been decided on the basis of intellectual property. The fact that a virtual gold piece is at some point rendered onto a chip of random access memory makes the case about the copying of intellectual property, or so said the court in *MDY Industries, LLC, v.*

Blizzard Entertainment, Inc. (2010).[19] No court has ruled on whether the software-use contract between the user and the company has anything to say about the legal status of the property within the game.

Nor have they ruled on the status of virtual money. As with rewards programs and FFMs, the first legal question that seems to arise about virtual money is not whether it *is* money but whether receipts of it are taxable income.[20] On one hand, the law says that noncash accretions to wealth should be taxed. Thus gold pieces, even if not considered money or cash, generate a tax liability. We have already seen that barter creates a sales tax liability as well. But in a 2007 paper, the legal scholar Leandra Lederman points out that wealth obtained through effort, such as fish hauled from the sea, is not taxed until it is sold. Apples are not taxed when you pick them, only when you sell them. Applying this reasoning to virtual worlds and social media would suggest that anything gained in a virtual world is untaxed unless it is sold for out-world money. Another legal theorist, Bryan Camp, argues that while this makes good sense in some contexts, such as games, it is less sensible in others. You could imagine, for instance, a virtual world where mother corporations trade finished products for raw materials with their subsidiaries using virtual currency, thus gaining a complete tax shelter.

Thus—is virtual property *property*? Yes. Should it be treated under the law as property? Maybe, sometimes. Until now it has been treated as intellectual property, but the main questions of real property have not been addressed. How does this relate to virtual property as money? It doesn't. Nowhere in the literature or the law has the connection been made between virtual currency and legal money, although by the time this book is published, there will surely be legal analysis of the issue if not actual court rulings. As I write this, however, there is no solid analysis.

GAMBLING AND SPORTS LAW

Perhaps we can find a legal home for virtual money in gambling and sports law.

Many of the economic activities that occur within games and social media environments involve some sort of lottery. The user performs some action and receives a reward that varies at random. In Korea and Japan, courts recently ruled that loot drops and the like from virtual world games constitute gambling and ought to be regulated as such.[21] Some state codes in the United States could be interpreted this way; the language is clearly broad enough to include virtual world items.[22] So what is the legal status of a poker chip? Apparently, the chips are owned by the casinos and cannot be used as monetary instruments outside their premises. Only the issuing casino can redeem them, and only for a limited time. Consider the story of Nolan Dalla, who in 2007 was given a $5,000 chip from the MGM Grand in Las Vegas by a friend. When he went to the casino and tried to redeem the chip, he could not prove to the casino that he had received it as a reward for gambling there. So the MGM Grand seized the chip. According to an article in the *Las Vegas Sun*, the casino was within its rights: Nevada law defined chips as casino property and banned their use outside the casino.[23] The piece also says that the Nevada rules were passed to bring the state into compliance with "federal rules prohibiting the creation of new currencies."

There are no such rules (or at least no clear ones). The piece also mentions a desire to bring regulations in line with "existing casino accounting procedures," which strikes nearer to home. If the casino chip were money, would there not be an income and sales tax burden generated every time man gave chip to man? It is in the interest of a casino to have its own internal money, but only if the money is not legally money. The law of Nevada was adjusted accordingly.

Rhode Island law considers trading stamps and coupons that are redeemable only for something random to be a lottery and thus illegal. Here the issue appears to be not the casinos' monetary health but the state's. In the United States, individual states exercise a monopoly on numbers running: only the state can operate a lottery. One can easily imagine someone running a lotto where the tickets are bought with something other than money, say a token or coupon (a casino chip?). Rhode Island law prohibits that.[24]

In the world of gambling, then, token money is considered completely legal—as long as the tokens are not used as a general form of currency. Gambling with real money is heavily regulated; gambling with tokens is accepted so long as the tokens do not substitute for real money.

Gambling law seems to permit a separate economic sphere, a magic circle in which the economy of a casino or a game operates freely. The law puts a boundary between the gambling economy and the outside economy. The law puts similar walls around sports. Lastowka offers illuminating parallels between sports law and virtual goods.[25] He gives the example of Dale Hackbart, a football player injured during a game who later filed suit against the other team for assault. The first court overruled Hackbart, saying that the football field was a place where the normal rules of assault don't apply. An appeals court then granted the suit, saying that while the rules of football are different from the rules of walking down the street, there *are* rules. In this case, the player who hurt Hackbart had broken the rules of football. The ruling thus gave legal standing to game rules. Later, however, in a case of a disabled golfer who wished to use a golf cart while playing, the U.S. Supreme Court ruled that the real-world law trumped the rules of the sport. But it was a tightly reasoned case; the court thought long and hard about what the game of "golf" was supposed to be, and whether riding in a cart was an inherent violation of its central spirit. In the end, the court ruled that golf was about hitting balls into holes, and that a rule preventing riding in a cart was not central enough to the sport to override equal-access laws.

The courts thus do consider the rules of a game and their centrality to the game's spirit. This is proper but messy. It tells us little about whether a game currency can be legal money. Is it essential to the spirit of a video game that its currency be (or not be) usable to buy movies and songs? If the game is about dragons, perhaps not. But what if the game is about running a virtual flower shop or trading in the stock market? Or international currency arbitrage? Would it not be central to the spirit of a game about trading virtual yen for virtual euros that you could also exchange the virtual yen for "real" yen?

THE BOTTOM LINE: WILDCAT CURRENCY IS LEGAL

The history of quasi-money in the United States leaves it unclear where most wildcat currencies fit within the law. Are they like casino chips, or like private money? Given the central role that money plays in the modern economy, the question has received surprisingly little attention. Central legal questions remain unresolved even as analysts describe the area as a "morass of federal and state laws, regulations, and rules."[26] There is no general legal framework governing the currencies now emerging with such explosive frequency. Later I will suggest the basis for such a framework, but for now, since no law expressly forbids virtual currencies, they appear to be completely legal.

4

IS IT MONEY?

We have seen that virtual currencies are apparently legal; there is no law clearly preventing a person from making up a new form of money and getting people to use it. In fact, many people are doing exactly that. But are these currencies actually *money*? It could be that folks are creating social media entities that they like to call money but aren't.

The textbook definition of money is simple. Money serves three functions, as a medium of exchange, a unit of account, and a store of value. Yet almost anything can perform these functions. Whales could be money; so could imaginary green ponies. In the tug and play of human trade, however, certain goods emerge as money more often than others. Economists would argue that these things perform the core functions of money better than others.

I think there is more to it than that. A thing becomes and remains money through a process of social equilibrium. It is money when we commonly agree that it is money. When we do, that thing serves the three functions by which money is defined. It is not those three functions that make a thing into money; it is rather a social process that enshrines a good as a unique artifact called *money*; once enshrined, that artifact serves money's three functions, well or poorly. There is no reason that virtual money cannot serve these functions. If a social process anoints virtual money as money, it will be money. There is some evidence that this is happening.

In this chapter I will make this argument in three steps. First I'll discuss the textbook functions of money and add a fourth function— the provision of joy—that has been overlooked. Then I'll look at the social process by which a good becomes money. Then I will assess the extent to which virtual money serves the (now) four core functions of money.

THE TEXTBOOK DEFINITION OF MONEY

Money is not a thing in itself; it is a label applied to a thing. A cigarette is always a cigarette, but at certain times and in certain places, it can also be money.

Traditionally, we would identify a thing as money using the definition in the economics textbook.[1] According to the standard usage, a thing is money when:

1. It serves as a medium of exchange. People trade stuff for it, not to use it but to trade it away for other stuff.
2. It serves as a unit of account. When people talk to one another or write contracts, they use the money thing to

express value. A thing is money when it is the unit used to the answer the question "What is that camel worth?"

3. It serves as a store of value. If people gather units of this thing and put them away somewhere, intending to bring them out again later and use them to buy stuff, then the object is being used to set aside value against later needs. It is a way to retain purchasing power through time.

The textbook definition, while functional and descriptive, says nothing about what sorts of items can serve these functions, or whether any should or should not serve them. It says nothing about whether money is "backed" by something else, as in paper money that is "backed" by gold. Cigarettes in prisons are not backed by anything yet serve the three functions adequately. Nor has the definition anything to do with law. A thing can be money without having legal status as money.

The textbook definition is careful in the sense that a good has to meet all three criteria to be called money. A share of common stock is a store of value but not a unit of account or medium of exchange. It gets traded now and again, but you can't simply walk into the yacht store and offer them a thousand shares of Apple stock for a boat. Full-time equivalent labor units (FTEs) are a way to express the comparable values of human resource investments, but you can't use a year of someone's labor to buy a car, nor can you set it away to use later (work disappears as soon as it is produced). Ration cards in the past century's world wars were used as a medium of exchange, but the unit of account was the underlying currency. Because these wars were expected to last no more than a year or two, the ration cards had no role as a store of value. All of these things resemble money in some respects but do not meet the full definition.

Defining money in terms of its functions may confuse you if you have unconsciously seen money as first and foremost a thing of value. We are born into societies in which there is generally only one metric of material worth. It is natural in such circumstances to believe that this thing is defined by the fact that it is valuable. Yet value or worth— or *utility*, to use a term favored by economists—is too tricky a concept to be used to define money. In a given moment, in a given society, it may happen that one particular object is seen by all as the most important material thing to possess. It is common to think, "Money is valuable to everyone, and it is the value that defines it as money. Money is the thing everyone wants."

Yet value is entirely subjective. Just why someone desires a particular thing is a matter of deep psychology. Sometimes the desire stems from an evolutionary drive, for food or sex or shelter. Sometimes it derives from social climbing and the desire for reputation—which may also be an evolutionary impulse, but not quite as old and deep as the drive to eat and mate safely—or is a product of addiction or false assumptions. Thus value is assigned to wildly different things at different times and places. Amber was once tremendously expensive because it was thought to have magical properties (if you rub it long enough, you get a spark). There's a thriving market for rhino horns because they are widely believed to be aphrodisiacs. For some reason, there is currently a positive price for photoprints of an individual named "Justin Bieber"; it defies all explanation. Meanwhile, some things that ought to be incredibly valuable have low prices. Where I live, water is very cheap even though humans cannot live without it.

Economics explains these phenomena through a subjective theory of value, which takes the tastes and desires of people to be unknowable. They are, of course, knowable, but economics cedes that ground to psychology. Economics begins only when people express their desires in markets. As buyers, people wish to purchase a certain amount of a good at a price stated in terms of some other good. When the price rises, this wish declines. Meanwhile, on the other side of the market, suppliers express a willingness to part with a good that they own in return for a payment. As the payment rises, their willingness to part with the good rises as well. If we add up all the wishes to purchase and compare them with all the willingness to part with goods, we will find that one or the other is larger. If the demand to buy things exceeds the willingness of people to part with them, the price of the items must rise. The rising price chokes off some of the demand and elicits more willingness to supply. If the opposite situation holds, if supply on the market exceeds the desire to purchase things, then a falling price will reduce the amount supplied while increasing the amount desired to purchase. Somewhere in the middle is a spot where the desire to purchase things roughly matches the willingness to give things up. At this price, deals may be struck that leave both parties satisfied. We as outsiders call this price the "value of the object."

This process is completely independent of any objective notion of the underlying value or importance of the goods being traded. They could be coconuts and apples, ships and sealing wax, or sex and drugs. Anything that can be owned and exchanged can be part of a market. Market forces determine the terms of exchange. No one person has any control over them. While I may believe that water is incredibly valuable to me personally, that belief has hardly any influence on the price of water in my town. The price is determined by the terms of exchange; the terms of exchange are determined by the balance, across all society, between people who want more of the thing and those who want less. The wanting of more and wanting of less is a matter of purely subjective judgment and is inexplicable unless one delves into the specific psychological and social properties of the good in question—terrain that is off limits for economics. Economics proceeds on the understanding that the value of things, as expressed in their prices, is at bottom a matter of subjective judgment.

Understanding this was an important step in the development of economic thinking, taken only in the late 1800s. Before then, economists had tried to tie the market price of a good to some kind of objective value, such as the number of labor hours required to produce it. If such a line of causation were reasonable and stable, it would also be feasible to consider that money was the most valuable thing in a society because it was crafted from some very precious metal or an extremely scarce item of great use. But it is not. There are goods that take forever for people to make that cost almost nothing (community theater productions) and items that people hardly work on at all that are very expensive (luxury shampoo). Similarly, in the realm of money, there are monies based on valuable objects and monies that are just slips of paper. We return again to the fact that value, as observed in society, stems from the impersonal working out of social forces driven by the desires, crazy or not, of average people. Similarly, the label "money" is applied to any object that, by an impersonal social convention, has come to perform three critical functions in society.

This historical three-function thinking about money may be in need of revision. We have seen in the game and social media industry that money plays an important role in entertainment. Could it be that money has a fourth role? Consider the possibility that a fourth function of money is to provide joy. One could make an evolutionary argument for this: our brains seem to be hard-wired to understand that abstract tokens can give access to material goods. It seems to be universally true that once an object has been accepted by social convention as money, having it provides pleasure. This pleasure in possession has nothing to do with the object's uses. The mere fact that it is money makes having it pleasurable. Obtaining even symbolic money activates pleasure centers in the brain. This is obvious to anyone who has played Monopoly—one of the commonest moments of happiness comes when a player passes Go and collects $200.

We might identify a joy function of money: money is our score in the game of survival, and we receive a jolt of happiness when we get it. I will say more about this in Chapter 5. For now, let us note that people count their money for no other reason than that it feels good to know how much there is. The pleasure people take in their money means that the development of virtual currencies has serious implications for human well-being.

MONEY IS A CONVENTION

The textbook definition of money points away from specific properties, items, and laws and says instead that money is an object that serves certain functions. How does a specific object come to serve those functions? I will argue that a good becomes enshrined as money through a specific form of social equilibrium called a convention. It is by a social agreement, a set of common norms, that a thing is accepted as a medium of exchange. Only through that agreement can an object be used as a unit of account—the thing traded for all other things—and therefore be used as a shorthand of value. And it is only because the social agreement persists that a thing may be a store of value: you can put it away one year and bring it out the next, and still have it accepted as a medium of exchange. Social agreements endow a good with the functions that money is said to serve. Thus conventions turn ordinary (or extraordinary) artifacts into money.

Conventions have been studied through the lens of coordination game theory, a subset of the area of game theory launched by John von Neumann in 1945. This is not the place for a treatise on mathematical game theory, but I need to explain the concept of a coordination game because it is the best way to understand why money is defined as it is.[2]

Imagine a game with two players. Each player has two cards, a red one and a black one. Each player chooses one card in secret, placing it face down on the table. They say "one—two—three!" and reveal their cards. If the cards match—red/red or black/black—each wins one dollar. If the cards don't match, each loses a dollar. The players win if they can coordinate their choices. If they fail to match the other's move, they lose.

Coordination games appear everywhere in life. To dance is to engage in a coordination game (in my case, a lack-of-coordination game). Driving is a coordination game: if everyone chooses to drive on the right side of the road, with "right" defined from the perspective of the individual driver, there will be fewer accidents. If we meet on the road, my driving on my right is perfectly coordinated with your driving on your right; since your right is my left, we will drive on opposite sides of the road and pass without hitting. We both win. Similarly, if everyone chooses to drive on the left, we win again. If drivers fail to coordinate—if some people drive on the right and others on the left—everyone loses.

Note the critical role of expectations in these games. I drive on the right because I expect other drivers to do the same. They expect the same of me and all other drivers as well. Since we all expect everyone to drive on the right, there is only one rational choice: drive on the right and confirm the expectation. So long as everyone is somewhat rational and makes the same choice, the general expectation of right driving will be confirmed by observation: most everyone in the United States drives on the right all the time. Except for accidents and madness, ours is a right-driving world. But suppose something happened to shake your expectations. Suppose the White House announced that next Wednesday is Left-Driving Day and conducted an extensive campaign to get everyone in the country to drive left for that one day. Perhaps it is a day of empathy for the wrong-driving people of England, Australia, India, and Japan. On that Wednesday morning, we would all wake up wondering what everyone else is going to do. Will they really drive on the left? Will I? What do I expect? My expectations will determine where I drive at first, before I see any other people. The same is true for everyone else. The whole country would be calculating what they expect everyone else to do, and choosing accordingly. Then perhaps when we actually hit the road we might see, in some places, that most people are out there left-driving. We would conform, and go left that day. In other places, left-driving might not take off at all. The boundaries between left-driving and right-driving cultures would be unhappy places where confused expectations lead to poor social coordination.

Another famous coordination game is called the Battle of the Sexes. Two people who love each other want to go on a date. The options are boxing or ballet. He likes boxing, she the ballet, but both would rather do something together than be apart. They both lose if he goes to boxing and she to ballet. They both win if they can coordinate on one event. But the event they coordinate on matters in this case, because the boy wins more if they coordinate on boxing and the girl wins more if they coordinate on ballet. Battle of the Sexes is an example of a coordination game with conflicts of interest. A real-world example occurs with principles like standards—using English as the language of business is favorable to those born in English-speaking countries. It is valuable for all business people to have a common language, but the choice of English, as opposed to Mandarin or Cajun, has distinct positive and negative consequences for different people.

Coordination games are a way to think about culture in general. Anthropologists refer to culture as a map of shared meanings. Things themselves have no meaning until we encounter them and treat them in certain ways. When those treatments are shared and persistent, they endow the objects with meaning. We see the meaning by observing how people act and speak differently in reference to objects and experiences in question. Two pieces of wood laid across one another are, to some, a Cross, and as a Cross the wood pieces will signify a massive set of shared meanings that have persisted across many centuries for billions of people. The two pieces of wood may inspire all kinds of behavior. These behaviors would not be observed, and meanings would not be persisted and shared, if people did not coordinate their reactions to the objects. If one person understands the two wood pieces as a religious artifact and another sees them as firewood, there's no shared behavior there. One person kneels to pray, the other lights a match. Being at cross purposes (sorry), the behaviors do not signify to others what the wood's meaning may be.

Money is clearly the result of a coordination game. The only reason money works is that it is accepted as a means of exchange, a store of value, and a unit of account. All three of these functions succeed only because we expect other people to treat money as having the value assigned to it. If those other people fail to perform accordingly, money will not serve those functions. When I hand the clerk a dollar bill, I expect that she will not squawk if I leave the store with the diet beverage I took off the shelf. If someone gives me a dollar bill in return for something, I am comfortable receiving it as such—even though it is a mere slip of paper—because I expect others to receive it the same way. The same holds for storing value and expressing the worth of things. If we all share expectations about the monetary functions of an object, then that object is money.

Think, however, what happens if we do not share these expectations or, as is more common, the expectations about money erode. This is precisely what inflation is: a gradual negative change in the shared understanding of what a single piece of money is worth. In modern economies, the value of the currency erodes by a few percent each year, for reasons having to do with macroeconomic management and the need to keep the wheels of the economy greased. The change is not announced or imposed, it just happens.[3] The people who manage the money try to make sure that the year-to-year change is too small to be noticed. But look back a decade or two and you may be surprised at how the value of money has changed. In the 1940s, in the United States, you could buy a roast beef dinner at a diner for less than a dollar. Today such a meal costs about $10. The dollar lost a quarter of its value between 2002 and 2012; cheeseburgers that cost $5 at the turn of the century cost $6.25 today.

Such changes are not enough to make anyone panic. Wages and salaries also rise gradually. People generally find they can make ends meet. They work, they get some money, they buy stuff, and life goes on. Nobody notices that the amount of money in the cycle is constantly going up by a little bit each year.

Sometimes, however, social expectations about money change extremely rapidly, and everybody notices. Indeed, they not only notice but panic. These episodes are sometimes called "hyperinflation," the prefix indicating an inflation that exceeds normal bounds. The classic modern example occurred in Germany in the early 1920s. That country had just been defeated in World War I, and the terms of surrender required the Germans to make reparation payments to France. The payments were simply too large and had to be renegotiated several times during the 1920s. Early on, however, France was quite insistent, and the result was intense wrangling over what would be paid and in what form. At one point the French actually occupied German territory and seized coal and other goods. The German government—Social Democrats, people who had had nothing to do with the war—had very few tricks to play in this game, but one of them was to devalue their own currency, the mark. This would reduce the value of any reparations paid in marks.

When the German government decided to devalue the mark, it did so with a vengeance. Within a very few months, from 1922 to 1923, the mark went from being one of Europe's main currencies to being a worthless scrap of paper. The tale has been told of a woman who took a basket full of paper notes to the store to buy a loaf of bread. The basket was so large it could not be carried into the shop, so she put it on the walkway outside. When she returned, someone had taken the basket—but left the money. During the hyperinflation, workers received wage increases several times a day. Prices at stores changed just as rapidly. A standard bill in the hand had a denomination not of 10 or 20 marks but 500 million.

Although severe devaluation was state policy, it was popular expectation that turned this policy into a hyperinflation. The government pumped currency into the system, but this, indirectly, made people believe the currency was valueless. Once people became aware that the currency was losing its value, the loss became an avalanche leading to a complete collapse. A shopkeeper who has seen the price of bread rise 10 percent a day for several weeks begins to believe that the money he makes will be worth nothing in a month. Says he, "If I am being paid in worthless money, I had better be paid a lot of it!" So he raises his prices as well. Monetary policy and loss of confidence fed on each other to erode the mark's purchasing power.

Thus a significant element in the managing of money is mass psychology: the managing of expectations about the currency's stability and future value. So long as everyone believes that the money is the money, it will be. If people begin to doubt that a given thing is money, or will be money in the near future, that thing will begin to lose its worth as money. The former money's buying power can keep falling until its price depends only on its value as a commodity. For paper money, this lower limit on value is zero. Money managers are therefore managers of a social convention, and their goal is to keep the convention hovering around a money value that is positive and stable.

VIRTUAL CURRENCY AS MONEY

If "money" is a label applied by social convention to any artifact that serves certain core functions, how does virtual currency stack up? Is it good money or bad? We can evaluate it according to each separate function.

MEANS OF EXCHANGE

To be a good medium of exchange, an item should be easy to use; it should not be heavy or hard to transport. Virtual currency fits this requirement wonderfully—much better than heavy gold or stacks of paper. It is weightless and can be transferred by sending bit-flipping messages through wires at light speed.

A medium of exchange should also be both divisible and aggregable. One never knows how small or large a transaction might be.

Virtual currency can be issued in any denomination or fraction, limited only by the numbering system of the database field it occupies. In principle, there are no practical limits on how big or small virtual currencies can be. They can be issued in any number of coinages with instant convertibility. For example, the game EverQuest lets you have copper, silver, gold, and platinum coins, with one hundred coins of any type being worth one of the next-highest type. Any nonplayer merchant would convert coins however you wished. In theory you could add Titanium, Metallium, Larrium, Moeium, Curlium, and so on endlessly. The possible range of values can serve an economy of any imaginable size.

The size range of gold is small. Minor transactions require tiny bits, which are hard to keep track of. Big transactions require wheelbarrows full of gold, which are hard to carry around. Economies that use gold must also employ metals of lesser value to cover a sufficient range. Paper money has a different but related problem. For big transactions, you either must carry around truckloads of paper bills, or the government has to print bills in very large denominations. But bills with large denominations are easily lost or counterfeited.

Counterfeit and fraud are the next criteria of exchange money. How easy is it to steal? As a digital asset, virtual currency is as easy or hard to steal as any other digital information. Is it possible to secure a database filled with credit card numbers? If so, then it is possible to secure a database that records holdings of virtual currency. Is it possible to securely transfer important information across the internet? If so, then it is possible to use virtual currencies to conduct transactions. The safety of virtual currency depends on the race between hackers and the guardians of information. At present the guardians seem to be in good shape. The amount of secure information on the internet is growing rapidly, and eCommerce companies are doing well. The ultimate test may be whether money stored as virtual currency is more or less safe than keeping gold coins under your mattress. Right now, that comparison favors virtual currency.

What about fraud? Setting aside stealing, how easy is it to trick people out of their money? Some kinds of tricks don't depend at all on the type of money. The Nigerian fellow who says he needs a business partner to help him recover a fortune can make the same plea in any currency. Counterfeiting the appearance of money, however, does obviously depend on the type of money. Metal money avoids counterfeiting by being dense and having certain properties (gold is not magnetic and is soft enough to show a mark when bitten). Paper requires elaborate printing and embedded materials to avoid copying. Virtual currency, being intangible, may at first seem immune, but it is easy to create a webpage that looks and acts like a real bank webpage. Here the thing being falsely presented is not the money itself but the claim to have money and to be able to transfer it. It's like faking a gold deposit slip. The slip says, "The bearer is entitled to retrieve ten bars of gold from Frank's Gold Smithy." But Frank's Gold Smithy does not exist. The website acts like a virtual money source but contains no actual money.

Barring a major update in the human condition, there is, alas, little hope for a decline in fraud. The opportunities for fraud and theft seem about the same for physical, tangible currencies and virtual ones.

Note, however, that this applies just as well to "real" money in digital form. Dollars recorded electronically in bank accounts are virtual currency. "Real" money in digital form is surrounded by high walls of security and reliability. It is tightly controlled and heavily managed, and of course performs well as a medium of exchange.

What about virtual currencies that are not the official currency of a state? Some of the considerations above change dramatically. For example, when it comes to theft and fraud, nonstate virtual currencies are certainly much less secure. It is much easier to fake the possession of a game currency than to fake ownership of a bank account filled with euros. It is much easier to hack into an entertainment company's servers than those of a multibillion-dollar international bank. On the other hand, private virtual currencies are just as divisible and portable as state virtual currencies.

Bringing the government into the discussion, however, raises another host of issues that all work to the advantage of nonstate virtual currencies as mediums of exchange. The state, as you may have noticed, taxes things. It tends to tax everything it can see, and what it can see depends on what is moving. Governments have found it easiest to raise revenue by requiring the reporting of any and all economic transactions and then applying a small fee to them. Sales have a sales tax. Registering a deed induces a registration fee. Giving a gift incurs a gift tax. Dying and leaving your stuff to others triggers an inheritance tax. Winning the lotto brings on a prize tax. But the diamond that sits on your mantelpiece is not taxed—it's not "moving" in the economy, so the state does not see it. If you sell the diamond, the state sees the transaction and may impose, in addition to the sales tax, a luxury tax on the buyer and an income tax on you for selling it at a profit.

Of course, the state is not just looking for things to tax but for evidence of crime and other bad behavior. Movements of money are the ants in a grassy field, signals for those who want to know the locations of anthills, the food sources, the threats, and how the ant colonies are treating one another. Knowing all this, a person may intervene to put the food in a fairer location, protect a weak colony from a strong one, or make sure that all the ants are competing fairly. The government may use information from money movements to gain revenues, but also to regulate commerce.

Whether this is a good thing depends on your politics. For good or ill, it happens. There can be no doubt that the impact of taxes and regulations is negative for those who feel them first. A pollution-control regulation that artificially raises the price of electricity may be wonderful for the air, but it depresses the market for electricity. It is in the nature of the free market that buyers and sellers of electricity would prefer to avoid regulation and conduct business at the lower price. If not for the government's regulation, electricity would be cheaper and more would be used. That is, after all, the point of the regulation—to cut back on electricity use and so cut back on coal burning, thus cleaning up the air. But users of electricity don't want to cut back, and the electric company does not want to stop selling sparks to them. To the people immediately affected by any tax or regulation, the main desire is to get out of it.

Nonstate virtual currencies thus offer a tremendous advantage as a means of exchange: the Great Government Eye may not see them. If I can sell my diamond to you in return for gold pieces from a game, which I will sell later for real money, we might just avoid taxes and regulations. If the government sees it all as play-money transactions, there's nothing for it to tax or regulate.

Whether you can avoid taxes and regulations and laws using virtual currencies depends largely on the reporting requirements. The point is that nonstate virtual currencies may be better means of exchange because they might allow buyers and sellers to avoid impositions that curtail exchange. From a pure efficiency-of-exchange viewpoint, virtual currencies allow more action for less burden.

UNIT OF ACCOUNT

The second function of money is as a unit of account. A good unit of account has a value that stays constant across space and culture (we'll get to time in a moment). The Canadian dollar is less valuable as a unit of account than the U.S. dollar simply because fewer people have a sense of what it can buy. A good unit of account can be easily expressed in numbers that people readily understand. It is very hard to grasp the difference between eleven trillion and thirteen trillion. Similarly, if someone says "My opinion is worth zero-point-zero-two dollars," it takes a moment to translate that into two cents. A currency's ability to respond to scale is critical, as is the communicability of the numbers.

Virtual currencies scale effortlessly. They can use any number system desired and can become known to as many or as few people as needed. Unlike systems based on seashells, rare materials, or large stones, a virtual currency is likely to be worth the same no matter where it is.

Does it matter whether the virtual currency is a state currency? For unit-of-account purposes, the backing of a government might make a difference, in that state currencies are more likely to be known and understood by a large group of people. Nonstate currencies may be more isolated, making the expression of value more difficult.

STORE OF VALUE

The final textbook function of money is as a store of value. A good store of value holds its purchasing power across time, meaning that prices expressed in that form of money do not change with the years.

A perfectly unchanging store of value is probably an impossibility. The prices of all things change relative to the prices of all other things. For instance, the price of computing power has fallen sharply over the past generation, while the price of a college education has risen. We can only speak of comparative price stability. This may explain why rare objects have been preferred as money; the scarcity of a rare object changes only slowly. But it does change. When Spanish and Portuguese explorers came back from the Americas in the 1600s and 1700s, they brought a lot of gold. Europe's gold-based money system suffered substantial inflation in that time period. But even if the rare object does not change, its terms of trade may change. If other goods become scarcer, the purchasing power of a piece of gold may fall anyway.

Imagine a desert island in which the currency is gold and the only commodity is coconuts. One hundred people live on the island; each cuts down a coconut every day and sells it to one other person. Everyone also buys a coconut from someone else and consumes it.

In Year 1, one hundred coconuts are harvested daily and there are one hundred gold coins, one per person. Thus each coin buys one coconut. A hundred years later, let's say the island population has fallen by half, so that fifty coconuts are harvested and eaten each day. But we still have one hundred coins: two per person. Now the price of coconuts will be two coins, not one. A man who stashed away a coin for his heirs would lose half of its purchasing power over the course of the century.

Of course it works the other way, too. If more people came to the island and the palm trees could bear the harvest, there would be more coconuts circulating and each would cost less than one coin. It is in practice impossible to guarantee that a given item will retain its purchasing power across time.

The only way to stabilize an item's purchasing power is to pay close attention to the relationship between the amount of the item in circulation and the total amount of trading going on. In real-world economies, matching money supply to money demand requires a vast regulatory and investment apparatus that works better or worse depending on the times. In game economies, it is a matter of faucets and sinks, regulating how quickly money flows in and flows out. Keeping money's value stable is a fiddly business, requiring constant updating so that the quantity of money matches the level of economic activity. In the real world there is a tendency to err on the side of inflation, always making sure there is a little too much money in the system rather than not enough.

All of this affects real money as a store of value. In the real world, savings opportunities have evolved to account for this gradual erosion property in money's value. A typical investment will have an inflation premium attached. For example, if the expected inflation rate is 3 percent and an investment is supposed to yield a 4 percent return, the stated interest rate paid will be given as 7 percent. When the investment pays off, in other words, the saver will get 7 percent of his investment as earnings, of which 3 percent is eaten up by inflation, leaving 4 percent as the investment's real earnings. If you would gladly pay me Tuesday for a hamburger today, and the price of the hamburger today is $10 but will be $12 on Tuesday, you'd better pay me $12.

Whether a virtual currency is a good store of value depends critically on its management. One is tempted to assume that state-managed virtual currencies retain their value better than privately run currencies. But the interests of states and private actors don't diverge significantly when it comes to managing money's value over time. Private companies can gain by creating a virtual item of value and then pumping out tons of it for themselves. States can also gain in this way. But they don't do it, because they have learned that the long-term loss of confidence in the money imposes far more costs than any short-run gains they might obtain. Nonstate currency managers must see things the same way. I could create a game in which the virtual gold pieces have real value, and then generate a million billion gold pieces for myself. But that would kill the game, and with it, my gold pieces' source of value. Both nonstate actors and governments have an interest in loosely managing money's value. It can erode and change, but it is best if nobody notices.

Incentives aside, technology and know-how favor the state-backed currency as a store of value. The state has ample powers to protect its currency from duplication, and ample experience doing so. Not so a small, new social media company. A currency run by twenty-somethings in a cubicle farm in San Francisco is much more vulnerable to accidentally producing billions of units overnight, or to having the parent company go bankrupt. Nothing is permanent in this world. The higher the chance that the managing entity won't be there tomorrow, the less useful the currency as a store of value.

THE JOY FUNCTION OF MONEY

Finally, there is the fun function of money. Can virtual currencies bring joy? Yes and no. People who play digital games greatly enjoy amassing virtual money in them. But perhaps something's missing: you can't run your hands through piles of virtual gold. If your avatar does so, do you get the same feeling?

The answer seems to be "yes." Owning virtual money makes people happy. I have played many games of many different varieties, and I can tell you, people love game money. They love working for it, hunting for it, killing for it. They love buying and selling for it, accumulating it in vast hordes, counting it, looking at it, and shopping with it. They love giving it away.

Almost every interactive entertainment product features some sort of money. Even single-player games typically have some sort of shop where players can spend some sort of coin to get power-ups. Take the single-player masterpiece for kids Plants vs. Zombies, or PVZ. In this game, you plant flowers that shoot peas at the undead trying to get into your house. You collect sunbeams to power the plants. If you kill a wave of zombies, you go to the next level. That's it; that's the whole game. Sunbeams, plants, zombies, level, repeat.

Now, when a zombie dies, it sometimes spits out a little coin. Click on the coin and it goes into your bank. At around level 5, your neighbor Crazy Dave invites you to look in the trunk of his car. He's selling gear.

This is where you use your money. You can buy seeds and power-ups and a rake for zombies to step on. It turns out that most of the things Crazy Dave sells are not critical to playing the game. Dave and his shop are unnecessary, yet there he is, hawking trinkets out of his hatchback.

This kind of reward system is common in computer and board games. On one hand, the player is rewarded for mastering the game. Puzzles are solved, monsters are killed, children are rescued, love blooms. On the other hand, the player gets some coin, which is then used to enhance the player's power in the core gameplay. It seems the designers make a fine game and then say, "Oh, and of course we will give them treasure and a store to buy things in." The assumption seems to be that players *want* money and a store. Do they?

Why would there be money in games that don't need it? Psychologists distinguish two kinds of motivators for action: intrinsic and extrinsic. We usually associate money with extrinsic motivation: If you want people to do something, pay them. Do not expect them to work for the love of working; instead, give them some reward for doing the work. We do not normally associate money with intrinsic motivation—the desire to do things just to do them. Here is the puzzle: people play games solely out of intrinsic motivation, yet the games have money in them. Does money satisfy *intrinsic* motivations? Do we pursue money because we just like money?

That is precisely what the evidence suggests. Psychologists Scott Rigby and Richard Ryan, who have done significant research in this area, point to three main elements of intrinsic motivation in games:

- Autonomy: the player feels free and his choices matter.
- Competence: the player feels that he gets things done and can master the situation.
- Relatedness: the player feels connected to a social world that observes and validates what he is doing.[4]

Money enhances all three. When a game gives you money and then invites you to spend it, you certainly feel more free and more empowered. In some political philosophies, owning property is the core requirement for being a free person. Money is perhaps the simplest indicator of autonomy. Rather than give players a thousand different types of gear they might feel good about, games give them one core metric of their autonomy: their cash balance.

Money enhances the sense of competence as well. Nothing expresses mastery like a big cash balance. Your money measures how many moments of domination and success you have achieved. Needless to say, games almost always start you out with nothing, and this is a powerful benchmark. "From nothing," you say, "I made all THIS!"

Money in games also helps with relatedness. When you have money, you have a reason to engage with and compare yourself to others. The relatedness motive works even in a single-player context; when you go to Crazy Dave, you break your isolation. Sure, he's not a real person, but research has shown that our brains react to unreal people and things in computers as if they were real.[5] Money gives you a motivation to go talk to somebody, if only to buy a rake for thwacking zombies. Meanwhile, that shopping moment makes you feel as though the money you've accumulated is noticed by others. Crazy Dave sells out of things, and it's because you the player are so darn rich that you bought out his entire stock. In almost all games, the player eventually becomes the richest person in the economy.

In my recent play of the game Skyrim, for example, my dungeon-delving was so lucrative that eventually I owned several houses and my (virtual) wife was able to wear the most expensive clothing and jewelry that existed in the world. My house was filled with luxury artifacts, and I owned horses, followers, and production facilities. I became the most powerful person in that world not just because I wielded the most badass sword but because I had the most money. Having money made me feel free, effective, and connected. According to Rigby and Ryan, I should be motivated in Skyrim to get money for its own sake.

Obviously, once you add real people to the mix, in multiplayer games and social media, these effects of money are only enhanced. In the research we did for this book, we found no examples—none—of a multiplayer online game with no money. Cash contributes to the fun.

But this is odd. Economies make a world more fun? Most people who have taken a class or two in economics generally find the subject oppressively boring. How difficult it must be to imagine that the presence of an economy makes a world more and not less interesting. How can this be?

Here we can point to the gap between experiencing something and thinking about it. I wager that thinking about economies crushes the mind, while living in real economies crushes the soul. However, *playing* with economies may be a blast. When we play with an economy, we gently massage all the elements of the mind that have been honed over the millennia to weigh options, to consider costs, to accumulate resources, to give gifts, and to make killings. Our minds reward moments of economic success with bursts of joy. They reward long-run economic achievements with long-lasting feelings of satisfaction. If the mind can be transported into a play economy, some shadow of these feelings can be obtained without putting anything serious at stake. We get the joys and satisfaction without the anxiety, stress, and bitterness often associated with economic success in the real world.

In games we also can act in the economy and learn its lessons the natural way, by making trades. The horrors of Econ 101 are avoided; rather than swallow dry theories, the student adapts by trial and error. Game economies thus navigate the narrow passage between the twin rocks of real economics and school economics: markets that teach lessons without killing you in the process.

Currency design plays a role here. So much of our economic motivations reduce to the accumulation and spending of "resource" generally considered. Our emotions do not reward us for the accumulation of specific items—for the acquisition of hazelnuts and dried meat—but for the accumulation of "stuff" and the proper husbanding of it. The human species evolved an incredibly varied diet and thrives in all kinds of terrain. This is no doubt implicated in a system of economic motivations that rewards the acquisition of resources in general and not specific things. Currency evolved as a way to denote and compare different bundles of specifics. It is a socially constructed metric of stuff, our general purchasing power, and our main metric of economic success.

As a measure of economic success, money seems deeply engrained in our minds, and we react strongly to its gain and loss. It would seem that the same engines that respond strongly to real money also respond strongly to virtual money. Wildcat currencies touch the same nerves as any other. Humans like money.

WILDCAT CURRENCY IS MONEY

It is clear that virtual currency can plausibly act as money under many circumstances. That said, virtual currency performs some functions better than others. It is an excellent medium of exchange: flexible, light, and divisible. It is a good unit of account: it can be known by all and scale to whatever size necessary. It is at the moment a poor store of value, largely because the private entities that manage it are less permanent than the modern state. Still, virtual currency does store value over shorter periods—years rather than decades— and in those periods it may be considered ordinary money. Many of the long-run implications of wildcat currency depend on the life expectancy of the currencies and the payments systems they support. Right now we do not know how long any of them will last.

PART II

IMPLICATIONS

The mix of social custom and technological change that is bringing so many new currencies into being seems unlikely to dissolve. We will soon live in a world in which anybody can issue her own currency and create her own payments system. How soon is impossible to say—but soon enough. Technology evolves rapidly, and by any measure the rate of change is increasing. Economic historian Gregory Clark argues that we should not think of our technological history as proceeding from a kind of Big Bang around the start of the Industrial Revolution.[1] Rather, technological development has been on an exponential path for many hundreds or even thousands of years. We were not conscious of it before because the amount of change within a lifetime was small. Around 1800, though, the amount of change within a lifetime became noticeable. Today, we are on the same technology curve that shocked Regency England, but it has grown ever steeper: change is apparent not in lifetimes but in years. The average twelve-year-old goes to school with more computing power than Neil Armstrong took on his voyage to the moon. In my pocket is a device whose powers in computing, communication, and information-seeking were unthinkable just five years ago. Today we call it a smartphone. In a few years, we will chuckle at that designation. "Dumb-phone," we will say. "It can't even render driving directions on my glasses." We've been forced to update our technological consciousness significantly in just the past five years, and we'll have to do it repeatedly throughout our lives.

In an era of frequent leaps in technology, leaps that always leave our technological know-how gasping for breath, we will always know that a new epoch is around the corner but we will have no idea what it is. The faucet of change runs too fast for the sponge of our society to absorb. There will be spillage and flooding and every possibility of big messes: lost advances, forgotten achievements, big mistakes. Technological surprise is now a permanent feature of human life.

The social change induced by technology has become chaotic in both the colloquial and the technical sense: it is a grand lightning ball of potentiality, likely to blow up at any moment in ways that we are unable to predict. Something will happen, but we don't know what. Rather than guess the future, then, the best approach is simply to be flexible. Flexibility, response, and adaptation in the face of currency change provide the theme of Part II.

5

WEALTH, POWER, AND HAPPINESS
THE EFFECTS OF COUNTING MONEY

Counting—basic evaluation—is the first and most obvious way that the emergence of thousands of virtual currencies will create social stress. Remember that one of money's core functions is to serve as a unit of account. How would we talk about economic matters if we did not have a common yardstick for describing what things are worth? Beyond its important technical role, money's accounting function also makes a critical cultural contribution. It is the way we keep score. Our magazines do not publish lists of the 100 Happiest People, they publish lists of the 100 Richest People. This may not be a good thing, but it certainly makes the counting of money important. That people are motivated by money means that counts of money affect how we behave. If we care about hard work, responsibility, investment, and economic growth, we should care how money is counted.

In A.D. 2000, the world had a few common yardsticks for its economic counting—perhaps just one. Values were expressed in terms of the U.S. dollar, or else the euro or the yen or the pound. It remains so as I write. A good argument can be made that the little wildcat currencies now popping up all over will soon disappear. To be successful, any form of money must cross a certain threshold of adoption. The more people use a form of money, the better it is as a medium of exchange. How can a wave of tiny currencies, being used by small numbers of people, possibly survive in a global currency system dominated by the dollar, the euro, and the yen? According to the theory of network effects, the biggest currency is the best and should wipe out its competitors.

At the same time, we do see many little currencies being used in odd corners of the economy, and massive digital value transfer systems have arisen. Moreover, the number of countries using the euro seems more likely to decline than to grow. Currencies do exhibit network effects, but they also serve unique local needs. The future of money is not monolithic.

The euro's tottering illustrates just one major concern about future value. A large share of economic transactions and contracts involve goods and services to be delivered in the future. Each such transaction requires an estimate of future values. These predictions are always risky, even when there is a single currency with low inflation. Uncertainties about the stability of currency add risk to all transactions involving future values. They thus have a systemic effect on the world economy: they can complicate the basic operations of states, people's individual motivations, and the ability of economic actors to negotiate now and in the future.

THE EVALUATION PROBLEM

Consider a basic and easily overlooked information problem that comes up in any society with material goods. What is any given object worth? This is the "evaluation problem." How can one person communicate to another the basic fact that this coconut, being filled with milk, is "worth more" than this empty one? The concept of worth must distilled somehow from people's behavior and translated into a simple, communicable sign. That is what money does.

Money is at the very root of material culture. If you know the prices of a society, you know a lot about its culture, desires, scarcities, and changes. This is powerful information. Early in the twentieth century, governments began to collect as much data as they could about economic transactions. Today, every government collects and reports on the goings-on of its jurisdiction's material culture.

This information is hard to acquire. Economic data collection requires hundreds of thousands of people to file forms, which are then pored over by machines and people to produce an unending series of huge reports. The reporting requirements imposed on private and public economic actors sustain entire professions, such as accounting, actuarial science, equity analysis, and public policy analysis. The evaluation problem is so big and important that we devote huge resources to just counting stuff.

How do virtual currencies affect evaluation? It might seem at first that they help. Virtual currencies leave a perfect digital trail. Every transaction using a virtual currency (including state-backed currencies in virtual form, such as debit cards) is recorded by a computer somewhere. It may not all be stored permanently, but it hits RAM somewhere and could be kept if desired. Thus one very exciting element of the future virtual economy is that every single economic movement of any magnitude whatsoever can be observed and recorded.

With the data being used for what? Imagine you had every byte of information about the global economy at your fingertips. Of what use would it be? Possession of massive data sets is a curse in disguise. This is illustrated by the story of Professor Dmitri Williams and his pursuit of data from the game EverQuest. In the early years of the twenty-first century, researchers had clamored for access to data from one of the large game worlds of that era. Eventually Williams was able to persuade EverQuest's makers to let him work on the game data files. These were duly dumped in his lap: a vast, jumbled trove of system inputs and outputs, arranged haphazardly in a massive relationship database. It was useless. Nothing recorded by the computers had been stored in a way that was intelligible to a human being. For example, the system recorded in one table every time a player paid the system two units of item 3382720 to buy item 999304298. Nowhere was it stated that the first item was a gold piece and the second a Potion of Minor Health. All such information had to be painstakingly re-created, and the raw data dump had to be rearranged, filtered, and aggregated into tables sensible to a breathing person. Two years and many supercomputing cycles later, Williams was able to begin studying the data, which proved to be tremendously fruitful. Dozens of papers came out of the EverQuest project.[1] Nonetheless, the story teaches us that simply having more data solves nothing. It has to be made sense of, and the more data you have, the more work goes into the sense-making. Having a massive trove of data does not mean you know what everything is worth.

That virtual currencies are all-digital and automatically recorded is therefore not as helpful as one might think. Furthermore, these currencies throw considerable sand into the works. It turns out that the evaluation problem is, at its core, a problem of expressing the values of different things in terms of common units. Even when everything in an economy is reported, that information must still be translated into handy and communicable units. For this, virtual currencies are a deal breaker. They replace a single common sign of value with hundreds or thousands of signs. This can only mean that we will have less usable information about our material culture as the currencies proliferate.[2]

A common unit is important because without one, it is impossible to think about the economy as a whole. No one can keep in mind the many billions of artifacts created and traded in a modern economy. We can think only in terms of big groups, like food, housing, and transportation. Yet there are millions of unique commodities in each of these groups. In order to build the category "food production," analysts need to add apples, oranges, coconuts, and caviar. The answer is to multiply each item by its price, so that you add money values. Food production is then the sum of the value of apple production, plus the value of orange production, and so on. This works so long as you know the price of each item in terms of a single form of money.

Thus if goods and services are expressed in multiple currencies, it is necessary to translate every item's value to some base currency that serves as a standard. To the extent that this is difficult or impossible, valuation itself is difficult or impossible, and with it, most forms of thinking and policymaking about the economy.

As virtual currencies proliferate, it will be harder and harder to know what things are worth, or for the state to report accurately on such basic economic indicators as GDP growth, balance of trade, and the amount of money in circulation. We will lose touch with the broader outlines of our material culture. We should plan for a future in which the basic values of things are a mystery. We have to be prepared to drop things that turn out to be junk and hold on to things that turn out to be priceless.

MONEY AND THE OBSERVATION OF THE ECONOMY

The implications of weak or vanished valuation are, well, really something. What if we did not know what enterprises are worth? What if the state could not monitor the economy?

SHADOWY ASSETS AND ENTERPRISE VALUATION

What would happen to global finance if it were impossible, or very difficult, to know whether a company is making a profit? One might assume that any publicly traded company wanting to maintain its share price would express everything it does in terms of a widely trusted currency like the U.S. dollar. But there are sometimes reasons to shelter value in obscure assets. Companies taking big risks have strong incentives to keep assets in nonstandard form and then make inflated claims about their value. If those nonstandard asset types are relatively easy to track down and account for, this is not a problem. If they are hard to find, hard to assess, inherently unstable, or prone to appear and vanish quickly, then their presence adds great uncertainty to the job of creditors and assessors.

Virtual currencies are just that sort of shadowy asset. It takes nothing to launch a virtual currency and trade in it. In game worlds right now, there is already user-friendly click-and-drag software for implementing a currency. It costs almost nothing to transfer units of a virtual currency. It is technologically feasible today for a company to create a new currency every year, conduct trades in it while it lives, and then when it expires liquidate the balances back into another currency. You simply have to generate a limited amount of a fictional unit that then temporarily serves as a medium of exchange, a unit of account, and a store of value. And if private companies can make a new currency every year, they can do it every month, every week, or every minute. Complex digital value transfer systems could be designed expressly to exhibit value when it is legal and expedient to do, and obscure it when it is not.

Doubtless there is some way to regulate this behavior, but it is hard to imagine how. A virtual currency can be named anything and thus hidden. Systems of multiple virtual currencies can be backed by translation tables that seamlessly translate one currency into another. If currency X is discovered and banned, the machines running the payments system can simply execute a protocol: "If a currency is banned, transform all of its assets into another currency." If a construction company's ledger reads "Bolts: +$2,395,343," this could refer to threaded metal rods, or to a virtual currency trading ring where the main currency is called bolts.

Assets denominated in virtual currencies will eventually show up on corporate balance sheets, and this will force everyone in the economy to consider what those assets, and the companies that hold them, are really worth. Even more, people will have to make judgments and act on them. To be ignoring virtual-money assets will be seen as very tweedy when everyone in shiny suits appears to be making virtual money on a minute-by-minute basis. The system will simply have to deal with the problem of assessing what operations in virtual currencies are really worth.

SHADOW MARKETS

The shadow effects of virtual currencies also represent a way for the economy to go "off-book" at levels never before seen. Some historical perspective is helpful. Until the digital age, the tendency was for the administrative power and competence of the state to grow, abetted by technological advances in communications. Through writing, books, and later telephones and computers, governments steadily increased their ability to know about things happening at small scales, and do something about them. The growth of administrative power can be seen in the growth of government expenditure relative to national product. This number was generally very small through the nineteenth century but now, in most developed countries, exceeds 25 percent of total national output. For one entity to control so much of an economy of hundreds of millions of people is possible only when it can observe, record, file, retrieve, and analyze data, and thus make decisions and send messages and officers to execute them. These two abilities, to use data and to send officers, have increased dramatically since 1900.

The observational and administrative power of the state made operating off-book unfeasible for companies of any size. Significant operations require significant internal reporting, which entails records and communications that the state can observe. Any effort to avoid the state means hiding lots of information.

The historic trend may now be reversing. What if the government's ability to intervene in the economy is outpaced by the ability of organizations, even large ones, to conduct transactions invisibly? The explosion of virtual markets (and other virtual arenas of human interaction) makes it conceivable that trades might occur in currencies that exist only for a few seconds. Like a black market that appears and disappears in an hour on a side street, virtual economies and their currencies may grow in some hidden corner of the internet and vanish in an instant. A huge fraction of trade may go off-book.

When trade goes off-book, it usually becomes more risky. Black-market economies are the Wild West. There are reasons why trade flourishes when it is regulated: contract enforcement and fraud protection. The absence of these trust-support mechanisms would ordinarily limit the size any black market can attain. But the same technologies that spawn virtual currencies could also spawn virtual trade-enforcement structures. In the multiplayer game League of Legends, players may report other players for vile conduct. A capture is made of the gameplay in the moments before the report. Players who have great experience in the game, based on their level, are then invited to review the captures and vote on whether a report was justified. They are rewarded for their time with game items and benefits. Is such an automated peer-trial system feasible at a large scale? Certainly. Wikipedia, Slashdot, and Reddit are all social media systems where things are competently judged and ranked by the crowd. There's no reason that recorded behavior cannot also be so judged. At the same time, automating and recording judgment means retrieving and systematizing behavioral data and making it available for scrutiny. This is exactly what the state would need to regulate behavior. Can a virtual justice system evade the state's notice? If so, there may be no limit to the size of the virtual shadow economy.

On the other hand, any shadow currency faces the problem of scale. An object retains value as money only if it is accepted as money within a group of people. A scrap of paper that I give to you has value as money only if you can give it to another person who also accepts it as money. It is not clear what social scale a form of money must attain in order to be trusted. If a currency is going to exist for only thirty seconds, is it possible to collect enough entities around the currency that it can be used to transfer value? If so, how many entities are needed? Perhaps any shadow currency system requires so many participants that governments will always be aware of the currency and thus be able to regulate it. It may not be possible to keep an economy "off the books" because, perhaps, only big currency systems work well. And no big currency can escape government oversight.[3]

I have no idea how likely these scenarios are. Whether a virtual black market sucks up much of the world economy depends on the strength of two competing institutions: state administration and the virtual markets. At the moment, virtual markets seem to be more powerful than the state. We may therefore see a large-scale exit from the above-board economy.

Such an exit would unleash other forces. Those left behind in the normal economy would have to bear the cost of the legitimate institutions of society. With fewer entities paying taxes, the taxes per entity would have to rise. This would only increase the incentive to exit, further reducing the tax base. It is a death spiral. Wildcat currencies may set off a general dynamic of state decline.

It is impossible at this point to know whether the evaluation difficulties caused by virtual currencies will be sufficient to let the economy slip out of the government's hands. The war between observing organizations such as the state and evading organizations in the virtual shadow economy has already commenced. An interested observer should be prepared for a major decrease in the revenue and power of the state.

MONEY AND HAPPINESS

There is more to the issue of counting than observation and control. Money is in many cultures a key measure of how one is doing in life. It's a way of keeping score. The joy function of money is one of its major contributions to human experience, and virtual money's potential contribution to human happiness should not be overlooked. State-backed money, though largely virtual in form, has never been used in a flexible way to promote happiness. But the pioneers of virtual currency generation are exploring wild new ways of using money to make people happy.

Research in the economics of happiness has turned up some interesting features of our emotional reaction to money.[4] First, we enjoy getting money and seem to have intrinsic motives for pursuing it. Second, though, we get used to receiving money. If we receive the same amount on a repeated basis, the joy it gives us tends to flatten out. To increase our happiness with money, we must get it in bigger and bigger chunks. This process, called a "hedonic treadmill," resembles an addiction. As with certain drugs, we can never get enough money. We always need greater amounts to get the same level of joy.

Consider a young man graduating from high school. He gets a job that pays $500 a month. Compared to his pocket change, this is major money! It is a wonderful moment. He buys things he could not afford before—his own apartment, a used car, better food, even a sit-down restaurant once in a while. Seeing that first paycheck feels so good! After some years, though, the paycheck goes into the bank account unnoticed. But if he works hard and gets a promotion, suddenly he is making $2,000 a month. Wow! A new car! A two-bedroom apartment! Eating at a diner every day! A trip to Florida! Still, a few years later, this lifestyle is not particularly noticeable. It no longer comes to mind that he has all this stuff he did not have before. The monthly $2,000 is, if anything, a barrier to further aspirations, no longer a joy but a reminder of what his dull life is like. If he gets a 25 percent raise, that's a good thing—but it's not amazingly good. And yet it is $500 more a month, the same he was paid what he got at his first job. He was so happy to receive that money back then, but now, just adding it to his $2,000 is good but not amazingly good. His reaction to receiving money has leveled off. I am sure that most readers have had the same experience.

Other aspects of happiness are not subject to this pattern. Happiness research suggests that a good family has a constant, sustained, and large impact on happiness. So does a long-term friendship. As for work, it is not the money that makes us happy but rather the vocation. Having a mission makes us happy for as long as the calling lasts. Money, the research shows, is just not comparable to these things in terms of long-run life satisfaction. Your best bet for a happy life is to marry happily, have children, and make friends; then stay put, spend time with these people, and pursue your quests.

MONEY AND MOTIVATION

Where did this specific pattern of money and emotion originate? Consider the evolutionary process that built our brains. We are descended from human beings who acquired resources of food, security, warmth, and mates. More importantly, we are descended from those who were better at acquisition than others. Resources are scarce. Sometimes there was plenty to go around, but at other times, some people got enough resources to survive while others did not. We are descended from the former. A basic drive to acquire stuff from the world has obvious survival value.

Humans are also a social species. Trading and sharing have existed as long as we have.[5] We have an innate understanding that one good can replace another; survival requires not specific amounts of specific goods but rather a more generalized heap of things, some consumed directly, others traded and shared. Getting a jolt of happiness from acquiring something that we can use or trade to others in our social world also has obvious survival value.

Why does this jolt of happiness go away? Imagine a survival environment inhabited by two early hominids, Joe and Frank. Joe likes to pick berries, but Frank does not. Specifically, Joe's brain gives him a little shot of joy whenever he picks a berry, but Frank's doesn't. Because berries help these hominids survive and have offspring, Joe is more likely to survive than Frank. Over the course of many generations, the population becomes dominated by Joe's descendants, people who get a thrill from picking berries.

This explains why we are happy from gathering resources, but not why the happiness fades. Let's introduce another pair of early humans, named Jane and Doris. Both are descendants of Joe; they both get happiness from picking berries. Jane, however, eventually gets bored; her interest fades after picking twenty-five berries. Doris happily keeps on picking. While Doris keeps picking the same berries, Jane looks for something else to do. Certainly, there are other activities that might hold her interest, such as gathering roots or fishing in the stream. She might even become interested in picking berries again, but only if that involved something more. Twenty-five berries a day is boring, but what if she found a patch with hundreds of berries, and roots as well! That would be wild. Should Jane find such a berry patch, her joy would go up again. Jane's motivations encourage her to move beyond the status quo, and the new things she finds, whether better berry patches or alternative sources of food and shelter, will improve her ability to survive and have offspring. Boredom is adaptive because bored creatures explore, innovate, and expand.

The evolutionary significance of boredom explains why we are not happy merely to have money. Having resources is necessary to survival, and having a desire for things like money does confer an evolutionary advantage. But the desire to *increase* our resources confers an even greater advantage. A contrary desire, to be satisfied with what we have, almost certainly is an evolutionary disadvantage in a world where resources are uncertain. Those who collect no more than they need do not store anything away and may be out of luck when hard times come.

Evolutionary reasoning explains why we enjoy getting more money. To put it very simply: Our brains believe that money stands for offspring. Thus they motivate us to always get more, more, more. Getting more, of course, depends on counting, which depends on the accounting function of money.

VIRTUAL VS. REAL ECONOMIES: WHAT'S MORE FUN?

The accounting function of money has serious implications for well-being and motivation. People are happy and active when they can count their gains in certain ways. How do virtual currencies affect this?

The quick answer is that virtual currencies do a much better job of providing happiness from money than the real economy does. The virtual economy can be designed to allow all kinds of counting experiences. People in virtual environments can acquire all kinds of currencies for all kinds of things.

How does the real economy compare? It is certainly fun for some people. Anyone who has a Horatio Alger experience, rising from poverty to wealth, certainly experiences a great deal of joy along the way. The vast majority of people in a free market economy probably experience it simply because of seniority and education effects. In a market economy, the wage is tied more or less to a worker's ability to produce value for the person who hires his or her time. An immature, inexperienced, uneducated person will generally produce less value than a mature, experienced, educated one. As a result, a person's income rises with age. It is not uncommon for a person to retire earning much more money per year (accounting for inflation) than he did as a youth. In the United States in 2011, the median annual income was $10,518 among the 15–24 age group but $41,550 among those aged 55–64.[6] Anyone living this story in the real world will also get some happiness from it.

Nonetheless, when viewed from a virtual economy design perspective, the real economy has some critical flaws.[7] The prevalence of anxiety and fear in the real economy is a problem. Risk has an odd relationship to happiness. As media psychologist Annie Lang has shown, we tend to have fundamental predispositions when it comes to threats.[8] We generally have some desire to confront and even seek out risks, but at the same time, too much risk creates anxiety and stress. Whether the risk is worth taking depends on the reward. This takes us back to money. In the real economy, money is both the risk and the reward. We are driven to seek more of it, but in so seeking, we endanger what we already have. The confluence of fear and excitement that money arouses should be familiar to anyone who has considered a major career change. Similarly, investments in the stock market engage risk in the hope of a higher return. There is a wide variety of risk/return opportunities in the real economy, and of course, the higher returns are available only to those who are able and willing to take the higher risks. If these high rollers win, they become even richer. Or they can lose everything.

While some risk provides motivation and excitement, it is not fun to face dramatic risks of loss. In game and social media economy design, one rarely finds examples where a player can go down from a level once achieved. All success or failure is couched in terms of how far one progresses from the current point. You never lose ground.

This makes the system feel far less dangerous. Note that you can still lose relative ground; others may speed along while you stand still, and this certainly affects your happiness. But in absolute terms, you can never lose it all. One feels safe in a virtual economy. Comparatively speaking, the real economy simply has too much danger.

Second, the real economy is too arbitrary. Who can grasp all the bizarre rules, norms, and expectations that influence our path through the modern economy? The formula for real-world success has some obvious elements (do not punch authority figures in the nose), but much else is obscure. Often we discover what we should have done only decades later. Sometimes we discover, long after the fact, that the game was rigged against us from the start or that we actually had no idea what was going on. By contrast, virtual economies are finely honed to match rewards to skills, information, and interests. There is no economic injustice on a grand scale. In any virtual economy, a more or less obvious system exists, graspable by just about anyone, that grants rewards for certain activities and choices. Every individual is roughly aware of the road to wealth and has the basic ability to take it. Not that everyone becomes wealthy; far from it. In some systems, it is clear that only those with great skills will become the wealthiest. Those skills may be physical, such as reaction time in combat; strategic, such as the ability to plan; or social, such as the ability make friends and become a leader. In other systems, skills have nothing to do with wealth; it is only a question of time input. And some people have much more time to put into a virtual economy than others. When the people whose skills and interests are suited to a given world's wealth-generating systems do in fact become wealthy, no one cares. Inequality of outcome is generally ignored by participants in social media and game economies. They understand exactly how the wealth was earned, and they know the system was objective and fair. Every player understands that the wealth could have been his too—he simply did not have the required skill, or chose not to use it.

Whatever the route to wealth may be in a virtual economy, that road is not murky or capricious. It is open to all, and all the players know how it works. Do this, get that. This is a major contrast to the real economy, with its vastly more complex roads to success and the heavy significance of random factors and obscure restrictions.

Third, the real economy offers far too little autonomy. Our story of hominids painted them as independent gatherers. Very few people in the real economy have that much scope of action. We are and always have been embedded in dense webs of obligation. Yet one of the most striking affordances of virtual economies is the independence and autonomy they offer. You generally can build your wealth without approval or assistance from anyone else. You are your own boss. This is only a dream for many in the real economy.

Finally, the real economy does a poor job of managing money's hedonic treadmill. Too many people start poor and face an early game that is too frustrating to seem worth it. Others find that the game was beaten by Dad; they're already rich, it's boring, so they quit. In most virtual economies, everyone starts with nothing. But from there, the system carefully and gently provides easy ways forward. It gradually increases the challenge as the player becomes more skillful and knowledgeable about the system. The risks rise gradually along with the rewards, so that the player experiences a nearly constant stream of happy moments. Each success is followed by a new challenge that is more difficult, yet still doable. In the real economy, by contrast, the great opportunity or the great danger of one's life can come at almost any time, whether you are young or old. It is poorly matched to a person's position in life. Virtual economies do a better job.

For all these reasons, economies built around virtual currencies may be better for human happiness than the real economy. If so, a certain pressure will develop on the managers of the real economy. It will be as though the people were rising up and asking, "Why is your economy less fun than the economy in the virtual world?" Game and social media developers are launching new currencies, new payments systems, and new economies that provide motivations and satisfactions for their users and thus compete with the real economy for users' attention and productive work time. If game economies are more fun than the real economy, they will get more attention, work, consumption, and investment. If game and social media economies do the best job of tapping into basic human motivations around money, they will thrive. Money systems that provide joy will survive, and those that don't will go under. As a result, the conditions under which people acquire and count their money may be dramatically changed as virtual currencies inspire new modes of economic interaction in the world.

RISKS, CONTRACTING, AND MACROECONOMIC HEALTH

So far we've considered two broad aspects of virtual currency: its effects on the state's power to observe, and its effects on happiness. These are significant enough. Moving from a single currency system to a wildcat currency system may have a third major effect, on the overall health of the economy.

The wealth we enjoy today is a direct result of past economic growth. People living in the developed world are the richest people who have ever lived. (Pharaoh had no dentist, but you do.) Economic growth is good in and of itself, but it is also a necessary precondition for medicine, sanitation, police, safety regulations, the arts, public education, and poverty relief. We therefore need to be careful not to endanger economic efficiency.

A system of wildcat currencies may introduce grit into the wheels of the economy at all levels. Trading and negotiating about goods and services takes time, and anything that increases the time needed to strike deals slows down the system. Consider Paul in San Diego and Jessica in Vermont. Jessica has a surfboard. Paul has a parka. At the moment, the two goods are without value, gathering dust in their respective closets. Now let Paul and Jessica trade their goods. Paul gets value from the surfboard and Jessica gets value from the parka. Merely by changing the ownership of things, by pushing goods toward people who use them the most, the economy creates value. Suppose, however, that Paul and Jessica had to negotiate about the exchange. Maybe they don't completely trust each other, or they have to decide who is paying for differences in shipping cost. If the bargaining takes only a second, it is not an issue. But imagine what happens if they can't come to an agreement in a day, or two days, or a week. At some point, Jessica decides that getting a parka and getting rid of the surfboard are not worth the hassle of dealing with Paul and his demands. In this way, bargaining and negotiation costs can prevent the economy from creating value.

Economists say that the failure to create value is equal to destroying it: it's value we could have but don't. An inefficient economy is one that fails to get the maximum utility out of a given stock of resources. In an inefficient economy, we have a hungry man with a glass of water and a thirsty man with a sandwich, but for some reason they do not trade and therefore remain hungry and thirsty.

A single currency contributes greatly to economic efficiency. A clear standard of value is extremely helpful to any negotiation, and this explains why money has such powerful network effects. As more people use a form of money, fewer of them have to haggle. To see this, imagine having to buy a used car using wood from the trees behind your house. You might have no idea how much the wood is worth. Neither does the seller. You would have to go check it out, or guess. Researching takes time, and guessing creates risk, and both can kill deals. A single currency eliminates this part of the bargaining by giving both parties a common standard for expressing value. Instead of trading a car for wood, you trade wood for money and money for the car. It is the most efficient possible way to make deals, short of sharing a mind with other people.

When there are multiple ways of expressing value, one must first translate everything into one value. This was the situation once faced by people in Europe. Before the introduction of the euro, it was a major function of the banking industry to set up kiosks at airports and train stations so people could rapidly translate one currency into another. It was fast and easy, yet not without cost. When you exchanged money, the bank took a cut—1, 2, 3 percent, presumably to cover its costs of making the exchange. This was a direct loss for the economy. The people, the time, the paper, the land for the kiosks all could have been put to some other use, like making kites or fried potatoes. Instead, the economy used them to move slips of paper from one spot to another. That's inefficient.

Bad as that is, it's not the major inefficiency caused by multiple currencies. I remember driving through the Belgian countryside having neglected to check at the border on the relation of the Belgian franc to the dollar. That afternoon I ordered a meal at a nice restaurant and when the bill came, I was convinced I had just paid a fortune for the glassy-eyed trout that was not at all what I thought I had ordered. The fish and I stared at each other, two broken fellows. It turned out to be a reasonable price, but I really had no idea.

Having no idea what things are worth is the true cost of currency confusion. When people do not know what a currency is worth now, and worse, what if anything it will be worth in the future, a risk premium is added to the price of everything. If I am offered a currency in trade, and I think it will fall in value, then I will insist on a higher price. If I think that the currency may disappear in a year, I will demand a significantly higher price. It is as if my trading partner were paying me with stock from a high-tech start-up—who knows whether it will be worth anything in a year? Therefore he'd better give me a lot of it. Although we can easily see what the stock trades for in dollars today, we do not know whether that market valuation is stable. Even if we have computers doing all the translating (which is far cheaper than having bank tellers sitting in airports and train stations), a multiplicity of currencies still puts a drag on our dealings.

This is why traders and business people have historically pushed for the adoption of one or at most a few currencies. In an era of wildcat currency, everyone who deals in the economy will have to research, or guess, what a given currency is worth at the moment. Not only that, we will have to have to find out where and how it can be used, since not all currencies will be tradable for all goods, or at all times and places. The currency situation will be confused.

This will create jobs for some people, such as those who code and manage automated money assistants, but all that work is really a dead weight on the economy. In a more efficient economy, they could be coding and managing something else. It may be possible for automated systems to handle payments and costlessly translate all currencies into one another. Perhaps there will be an application that allows us to simply select one type of currency, and then all items of value that we encounter will be expressed in this currency. I imagine a little app that lets you drag coins of various denominations from a cartoony vault onto pictures of the things you want to buy. Someone would have to build and maintain such an application, however, and he, too, could have been doing something else. A world of currency confusion will impose costs.

THE EFFECT OF LOSING A MONEY STANDARD

When we move from a few standards of value to many, it may be difficult for the state to keep up, and this has implications for how large governments may be. We may see a transfer of productive labor into virtual economies because they bring people more happiness. And the economy as a whole may grind more slowly because of money confusion. In a wildcat currency regime, we will lose efficiency in some places and gain it elsewhere. We will probably gain autonomy on the whole, but the risks we face will shift. We will not have a single stable currency in our pockets, and because the state's ability to tax may decline, it may become harder for governments to insure us against poverty, accident, and the effects of old age. We may, however, be spending more of our time in economies that have a better design. Will we be happier? That is impossible to judge. Things will certainly be different.

6

CURRENCY AND CONFIDENCE

In the previous chapter we looked at money as a unit of account; in this chapter I will discuss some concerns raised by money's role as a store of value. This involves the mass psychology of money.

As we have seen, games and social media developers approach economic policy from a unique perspective: they want to make people happy and engaged. They thus operate under different constraints from decision makers in the real economy. One important difference is in scope. Each manager of a virtual currency considers only the health of her own company and the contribution of her currency to it. Because all national economies are interdependent, regulators of the real world economy must consider the health of the entire system.

Wildcat currency takes us back to the nineteenth century and before, when banks could issue their own money notes and manipulate their value. Today's virtual currency operators are in exactly this situation. It is worth noting that financial panics were not at all uncommon in the era of private bank money: the money system failed, usually dramatically, with some frequency. In Chapter 2 we looked at the basic mechanics of money creation and how it leads to genuine interdependence among financial businesses, so that if one fails the others do as well. Here my focus is on the broader issue of faith in money, and why wildcat currency might erode faith in the economy as a whole.

The entire economy rests, we might say, on trust: trust that people will do what they say, that the laws and regulations do not change capriciously, that the objects being traded are what they seem to be. Studies have shown that trust at the national level is an important foundation for a healthy civic society as well as for economic wealth.[1] Courts and governments are certainly important in supporting the institutions of trust in an economy, but they can do only so much. A society without trust is not going to become trusting simply because it has lawyers and judges and government officials. It is conceivable, on the other hand, that a trusting society could sustain trust for some time even if those aids were removed. Trust is part of the culture, which is a phenomenon of commonly shared meanings and understandings. Therefore: what is the mass psychology of money, how does it affect trust in economic affairs, and how will it be influenced by wildcat currency?

INFLATION

Let's begin with the concept of faith in a currency, for here we have a measure of the rate of change of general confidence: inflation.

Inflation, a technical economic concept, is widely misapplied in common conversation. In general terms, "inflation" means expanding, blowing up, getting bigger from the inside out. It is often applied then to anything in the economy that gets bigger—one might say that food prices have inflated, spending on cars has inflated, or the government budget deficit has inflated. These usages are unfortunate and confusing, because the term has a specific meaning in economics: inflation is a rise in all prices. It even has a technical measurement:

- Take a basket of goods and services.
- Find out what the basket costs in year 1.
- Find out what the same basket costs in year 2.
- *Inflation* is the difference in the two costs.
- The percentage difference is the *inflation rate.*

Inflation can be defined for different segments or sectors of the economy, or for the whole economy. The definition varies only with the basket of goods and services; if you include all of an economy's goods and services in the basket, you get an all-economy inflation rate. If you include only a subset of commodities, you get an inflation rate for the subset.

Money appears in the concept of inflation in a very specific way: it is the item in which prices are expressed. It does not matter what kind of money you use. You could express the cost of the basket in terms of a paper money that has no real use or purpose, or in terms of an item that is actually useful. You could even use an item in the basket. Suppose an apple costs two dollars. A basket with a dollar price tag of $2,054 could be expressed as having an apple price of 1,027 apples. A common practice in inflation studies is to consider the cost of the year 1 basket as one unit of a fictional currency; that is, the price of the basket in year 1 is simply 1. Then the price of the year 2 basket will be something like 1.04, meaning, "it costs 1.04 year 1 baskets to buy the year 2 basket."

Because inflation is about the price of all goods relative to a designated form of money, it measures a change in the value of that money. There is an equivalence between the idea of prices as a whole going up and down, and money losing and gaining value. When prices rise, money has less purchasing power, and vice versa when prices fall. The change in money's purchasing power creates issues of faith and trust. As the measure of how rapidly a currency is losing purchasing power, inflation also measures how trustworthy that currency is. A rapidly inflating currency will buy many fewer things in a few years, so you should not hold onto it. This is another way of saying you should not trust it as a store of value.

Why should we lose faith that a given piece of money will buy next year what it buys today? It seems a puzzle. Why, after all, should the prices of *all* goods and services ever change? Imagine an island economy. All we have here are coconuts and shrimp. We use seashells as money.[2] Because there are twice as many coconuts as shrimp, we see prices of ten shells for a shrimp, five shells for a coconut. Why would it ever happen that, a year later, shrimp costs twenty shells and coconuts ten shells? Or four shells for a shrimp, two shells for a coconut? Yet this happens constantly in modern economies. In the United States, the average inflation rate from 2002 to 2012 was 2.5 percent per year.[3] Prices were flat in 2009, but in every other year of the decade, they increased by at least 1.5 percent. Year after year, for some reason, a basket of the same goods gets more expensive.

The simplest explanation for inflation in modern economies is called the quantity theory of money, according to which there is a relationship between the amount of money in the economy and the number of transactions being conducted. If the number of money units increases more rapidly than the number of things being bought and sold, then the prices of all things rise. The quantity of money, in other words, determines the price level. In our island economy, we might expect the prices of shrimp and coconuts to rise if a big storm blew hundreds of new seashells onto the beaches. People would run down to the beach and get the new shells. Feeling rich, they'd then run around buying up shrimp and coconuts. These would go into short supply. Prices would be bid up. Because the underlying economic conditions have not changed—we've still got twice as many coconuts on the island as shrimp—the price ratio between shrimp and coconuts would remain 2:1. But the addition of new shells would fix that ratio at a higher overall level. The addition of new shells lowered the purchasing power of a shell.

Trust in money, therefore, is a question of how the raw amount of money in an economy relates to the amount of trading it supports. The quantity theory works well in a simple economy and is therefore useful in understanding virtual economies. Virtual economies generally don't have banking, finance, or government borrowing. Most just have transactions and money in a fairly closed system. When the people who run virtual economies pump money into them, prices rise, and the money loses value.[4] When the users of a virtual economy change their behavior to increase the rate of money creation without a corresponding increase in trading, the money loses value.

What about inflation in a big, complex economy? There, both parts of the equation—the amount of money and the amount of trade—are obscure, hard to measure, and harder to manage. There can be no doubt that the relationship between the amount of money and the number of transactions still matters. But things get fuzzy when we ask questions like What constitutes a transaction? and When is money "available" to be used for a transaction? This is not the place to go into the intricacies of monetary policy, but one thing is fairly clear: at some level of complexity, the determinants of the value of money extend beyond purely mechanical questions of quantity. Faith in the currency becomes important, and this is a matter of mass psychology.

We will see later how psychological categories like panic have affected the value of real things. For now, consider how mere expectations can affect the value of money. Consider the fact that paper money has no use whatsoever. You can't eat it, you can't wear it, you can't write on it. Its sole purpose is to be traded away for things that you can eat, wear, or write on. The value of paper money, then, depends entirely on what you believe you can get in exchange for it. When you go to the grocery store, you assume that you can get a loaf of bread for one dollar. Your belief is quite rational, because every time you go to the store and grab a loaf of bread, you can hand the lady a dollar bill and she lets you take the bread home. Your belief in the dollar's value is confirmed by the actions of others.

What produces these actions that confirm your belief in the value of money? It is their belief about your actions. The lady who owns the store takes the useless dollar from you and gives you useful bread because she believe that you, and others, will let her exchange the useless dollar for other useful things. You believe her, she believes you, and everyone believes everyone else. All share the common belief that a dollar is worth a loaf of bread. The dollar's value thus rests on a web of belief: "This useless thing can be traded among us for things of value, therefore, it can be treated *as if* it had value itself."

"As if." That's the critical leap of faith. The dollar bill has no inherent value, but we treat it *as if* it did. We do that because we expect others to do the same. It makes sense as long as enough of us share this expectation. The instant that we no longer do, it no longer makes sense to believe in the *as if*. If the lady at the store won't take my dollars, I will not accept them from others. If nobody accepts dollars as payment, nobody ought to. It would be like accepting blades of grass or clouds as payment for items of genuine value and scarcity.[5] Thus when expectations break down, the value of the money vanishes like mist. Expectations are ephemeral; they are in the mind. Thus if expectations can vanish, so can value. It can be present one moment and absent the next. If people change their notions of how others will treat a certain piece of paper, that piece of paper can instantly change from money to not-money, or from not-money to money. Such changes need not have anything to do with tangible reality. They are caused solely and entirely by a change in the way people think. The value of money is brittle.

Fortunately, expectations in a society do not usually change instantly. They change gradually, and this is what characterizes the inflation rate in most modern economies. Year by year, the standing expectation of what a unit of currency can trade for erodes by a few percent. It is almost unnoticeable, until you watch an old movie and see people paying almost nothing for gas and haircuts. When the erosion of currency *is* noticeable, inflation becomes a major political issue. When inflation rates in the United States approached double digits in the late 1970s, many people felt it as a genuine social crisis. Similar moods of decline and catastrophe attended the rise of inflation rates in South America to 20, 30, even 50 percent per year in the 1980s. Policymakers work very hard to avoid such circumstances. Yet they also avoid deflation of any amount. The ideal choice seems to be a low rate of positive inflation.

WHY SMALL INFLATION?

Why small inflation? Let's begin with deflation, which is taken to be disastrous. Deflation means that all prices are falling and the currency is gaining value. Why is this a disaster? Return again to the mass psychology of an economy. If you hold paper money and see that it is actually gaining in value, it may occur to you that you can increase your purchasing power—make a profit—by not spending it. Consider a commodity that in itself does not lose much value in a year: a barrel of oil. Say you buy a barrel of oil for $100 and hold onto it for a year. During that time, the currency appreciates by 10 percent, which means the prices of all goods and services fall by 10 percent. The oil does not change in value; it is just as useful, and just as scarce, as it was when you bought it. But its price falls over the year, from $100 to $90. Say you sell it, taking your $90 payment in cash. Nothing has changed for you, because the $90 now buys as many goods and services as $100 did a year ago. You have stood still. But what would have happened had you held onto the money instead of buying the oil? After a year you would be holding $100 instead of $90. The $100 now allows you to buy 10 percent more goods and services than it did a year ago. While the oil stayed flat in value, the money appreciated. It was the better investment. In times of deflation, it is smart to hang onto your money.

But if many people hold onto their money, this can dramatically reduce real economic activity and growth. When people don't spend their money but put it under their mattresses, businesses experience lower demand for their goods and services. The businesses must cut back or go under, so they reduce their spending on inventory and labor, canceling orders and laying people off. This causes more people, now unemployed, to cut back on spending and causes other businesses to follow suit. Spending reductions ripple across the economy in a chain reaction of economic decline. In extreme circumstances, the contraction can be so large that even though individual people are saving more of their money, the economy as a whole is saving less: savings is a bigger share of a shrinking pie. In this odd way, the best way to increase savings in such an economy is to encourage people to spend. This is known as the paradox of thrift: countries filled with thrifty people may have less overall savings. Not everyone adheres to this policy lesson, but there is broad agreement that deflation leads to economic contraction, with all its ills: unemployment, closed factories, reduction in public services, and worse.

High inflation can also be ruinous. As we have seen, when inflation is too high, people lose faith in the future spending power of their money. This loss of faith extends to other institutions, and periods of high inflation have often become periods of government crisis.

If high inflation and deflation are both bad, then low but positive inflation remains an acceptable middle ground. Low inflation is the target that economic policymakers have adopted, not because it is wonderful in itself but because the alternatives are so unpleasant.

MONEY, DEFLATION, AND INFLATION IN VIRTUAL ENVIRONMENTS

BITCOIN AND VIRTUAL DEFLATION

Game and social media designers seem to have reached the same conclusions as real-world policymakers. Though I have no firm statistics on this, I can say with some confidence, based on direct experience in numerous virtual worlds and social media environments, that deflation is exceedingly rare. Neither I nor my graduate students have ever encountered a player who has experienced a virtual currency deflation. Nor have we heard of one.

There is one virtual currency, the Bitcoin, that may be deflationary by design, though it has not experienced deflation yet. By design, the amount of Bitcoins in circulation is never to exceed a set level. Bitcoins are created through a protocol that involves huge computers grinding away on massively difficult problems. While anyone in the world can set up a computer to do this "mining," the fact is it takes a certain and known amount of time for any computer to solve a Bitcoin problem. Bitcoin-mining problems have been set up so that they get harder and harder every year, with the result that, sometime in the mid-twenty-first century, every Bitcoin that computers can conceivably mine will have been mined. The specifics of the Bitcoin protocol are complex, but it operates such that the mining problems of the year 2050 would require a computer the size of the entire universe operating at the speed of light. The day will therefore come when no more Bitcoins will appear.

Given this structure, the Bitcoin will generally appreciate. In a world in which the number of economic transactions is always rising, a fixed currency amount is eventually guaranteed to bring price deflation. To return to the island economy with its shrimp and coconuts, if we fix two thousand seashells as the money in the economy but double the number of shrimp traded per day from five hundred to one thousand, and the number of coconuts from one thousand to two thousand, the price of shrimp will fall from four shells per shrimp to only two, and coconuts will fall from two shells per coconut to one. Fixed money with rising transactions means the money price of each transaction must fall. Though the number of Bitcoins in circulation is rising as we write, it will not always be so. The long-run health of the Bitcoin economy will probably be compromised by the currency's inevitable deflation, which will encourage people to store their Bitcoins instead of spending them.

INFLATION IN VIRTUAL CURRENCIES

While Bitcoin seems to be the rare example of a virtual currency that will appreciate, there are many examples of excessive virtual depreciation. Some occurred by design, others by a combination of accident and players' bad intentions. One early example is from the social media environment Habitat.[6] An error in prices on automatic vendors resulted in a situation where users could buy Crystal Balls for eighteen thousand Tokens at one vendor and sell them for thirty thousand Tokens at another. One night, two players shuttled back and forth between the vendors for hours, amassing Token balances several orders of magnitude larger than the designers had intended. The system's money supply quintupled overnight. The owners did nothing about this other than quash the bug. The newly wealthy folks spent their cash on treasure hunts for the other users. The new money was not removed from the system; rather, the price level in player transactions was allowed to rise. A similar money explosion occurred in the game Ultima Online when an enterprising fellow figured out how to automate the mining of gold.[7]

These and other stories tell us that hacks and bugs and mistakes are a significant source of inflation in games and social media environments. Crafty players figure out how to make the system put more money in their accounts, then exploit the bug until it is fixed. If they share the trick with others, an immense amount of currency may rush into a system before the bug is quashed. This money, if not removed, drives up the player-to-player price level. These bug-related inflations have been common enough that virtual world developers devote considerable resources to securing property rights—that is, to making sure that every account owns exactly what it is due and nothing more.

The design flaws that create virtual inflation stem from the way designers put money into their worlds. In the real world, money is cocreated by the government and the private sector. The government can create money simply by issuing it and then using it to buy things, as when kings had their own mints, stamped their own coins, and used them in royal finance. In the contemporary economy, the vast majority of money creation happens when private banks accept deposits and then lend those deposits to other people. The person who made the deposit of one coin has a slip of paper that can be used as a coin's worth of money, and the person to whom that coin was lent also has a coin's worth of money. One coin, two coins' worth of money.

Games and social media environments do not create their money through banks. There are no banks. Rather, every user is enabled to safely and securely store as much currency as desired in what is in effect a perfectly secure vault. The services this vault provides are so perfect you do not even notice them. Not every virtual world operates in exactly the following fashion, but we have found few deviations from it: When you go to a merchant or a screen that says, STORE, a window called "Inventory" opens. It lists the things you own. Down at the bottom, there is a line that says "Gold: ####." You click on one of the things in your inventory and a dialog window opens that asks, SELL? with a choice of yes or no. Click "Yes" and the item vanishes from your inventory. At the same time, a number is added to the Gold line. If you want to buy something, you click on FOR SALE. Again a list of items appears. Click on one to buy it. When you do, the item appears in your inventory, and a number is subtracted from your Gold line.[8]

The line that says "Gold: ####" is the perfect vault, better than any real-world bank. It can hold any amount of money. You can access it at any time. It pays no interest. It charges no fees. It accepts orders to transfer funds to any person or entity without a second's hesitation and at no cost to either party. No shipping fees, no transaction costs. It is perfectly safe—or, more precisely, no more or less safe than holding things in your inventory.

You cannot borrow from this vault; it makes no loans but rather focuses on transactions and payments services which, as we said, it performs perfectly. This vault is not a profit-seeking entity; it is utterly unconcerned that there may be millions upon millions of gold coins gathering dust in its coffers. While it could make money lending the idle coins to others, it is designed not to do so. The vaults of game economies do not make loans, therefore they do not make the money.

HOW GAMES CREATE MONEY

How then does money enter the game economy?

One method is by royal fiat. The developers of the virtual world are kings. They create money in their databases and then have various in-world agents offer to buy things from players in return for money. Thus a fantasy game may have a merchant named Marvin sitting by the docks. You go up to him and click. The STORE pops up: "Welcome to the Den of Marvin! How may I assist you?" You can sell things in your inventory to Marvin, and he will give you gold coin—which he got from nowhere. The designers have given the Marvin robot the power to generate new money and transfer it to players. They control the money supply by setting the prices Marvin will pay for various things. If they want to inject more money into the economy, they raise his buy prices, and lower them if they want less money. They can also control supply on the selling side: by selling items to players, Marvin takes their gold out of the system. If the developers have him sell powerful goods cheaply, he will sell quite a few and thus suck a lot of money out of the system. By altering the buy and sell prices of stores, the designers can control the flow of money into and out of their economy.

A second method is by magic. A player goes into the virtual wilds and kills a beaver. Lo and behold, the beaver is found to be hoarding treasure! A piece of leather and two copper coins! These items go into the brave hunter's inventory, and the goods and money thus enter the economy. The leather counts as a harvest and makes a kind of sense: at least it's animal skin. What makes less sense, but is a near-universal practice, is that every living creature one dispatches in the world—not just dragons but also beavers and rats—happens to be carrying money.

The reason for this is simple: people get a hedonic boost from gaining money. If the purpose of the game is to kill monsters, then the act of killing a monster (even a small furry one with buck teeth) must be rewarded with treasure. In social media environments, coins reward other kinds of behavior: solving puzzles, chatting with others, achieving something in a casual game. The designers can alter the inflow of money by changing the "drop rate," the rate at which doing things in the virtual world generates new money.

This method of generating money has a negative counterpart: money can also be made to magically vanish. Usually this is labeled a fee or a tax. For example, if you go to a wagoneer and get a ride to another part of the map, the system deducts a certain amount of gold from your bank. When you sell something to another player, the system commonly takes a share of your proceeds.

While these deductions are not popular with players, they are necessary for sound money management. It is worth pausing for a moment to see how game designers accomplish it. The most common way fees are applied is through an auction house, which tends to run in the same way on all platforms.[9] At the auction house, any player may post an item for sale. When the item is posted, the system demands a deposit of 1 or 2 percent of the asking price. If the item does not sell, the deposit is usually returned (in some games it is not). If the item sells, the seller receives the sale price plus the deposit, minus an "auction house fee." This system effectively hides or at least obscures what is in fact a sales tax. The buyer pays no tax at all: he sees the price of an item, pays that price, and walks away with the item. The seller sets a price, pays a deposit that appears negligible, and receives the sale price plus a bit more. For example: Annie posts a magic helm for sale for one hundred gold. When she posts it, the system says "Deposit: five gold." She pays the five gold and goes on to other things. Three days later, she receives a note from the system: "Your magic helm was bought by another player. One hundred three gold has been deposited in your account." Annie may not remember the exact sale price she set for the item or the amount of the deposit. She is unlikely to realize she has just paid a 2 percent sales tax. Yet she has, and this is a way the designers suck money out of the economy. It is a powerful way of doing it, because the amount of money removed depends on how busy the auction house is. A busier auction house obviously removes more money from the economy, and a quiet auction house leaves money in the economy. This is interesting and powerful because a quiet auction may reflect a depressed economy, and you should not remove money from a depressed economy. You should, however, remove money from a booming economy; a booming economy needs to be settled down. The auction house system, like a real-world sales tax, is an automatic economic stabilizer.

It is striking how this system uses the same psychological tricks that governments use to get us to accept tax burdens. In many real-world income tax systems, money is automatically taken out of our pay, and then we must file forms to reconcile this withdrawal with our actual tax burden. The general practice is to withdraw more from a person's paycheck than she will actually owe, so that the annual form-filing results in the government sending a refund to the taxpayer. Unlike the withdrawal, the check is directly and consciously perceived by the taxpayer, so that it seems to be a benefit or gift from the government rather than what it really is, a correction of an inappropriate government seizure of funds. Real-world governments, like those in charge of virtual worlds, manipulate the timing and placement of their monetary policy so that people generally perceive only the parts that are likely to make them happy.

These methods of injecting and removing money from a virtual economy are technically known as faucets and sinks. Faucets put money into the system and include such things as loot drops and nonplayer merchants who buy player goods. Sinks take money out of the system and include such things as auction house fees and payments for services. The virtual monetary policy problem is to set the system's faucets and sinks to maintain positive but low inflation in the economy.

As virtual money systems proliferate, it is interesting to speculate on what this might mean for real world money. Imagine a government running things like a virtual economy, issuing money to people for free and preventing banks from making loans with other people's deposits.[10] It would be different but not unfeasible.

SPECULATION AND FINANCIAL PANICS

So far in this chapter I have been discussing the impact of price changes on real and virtual economies and tracing those back to people's core level of confidence in an economy and its managers. We can now consider how wildcat currency might affect the primary danger of all money systems, the risk of financial panic and collapse. As we saw, it has not been uncommon for types of money to suddenly lose value. In our current system, with a handful of major state-backed currencies, these risks are very low. These risks are very much higher in a wildcat currency system.

Recall from Chapter 2 the nature of a financial panic caused by bank notes: When a bank goes under, its notes lose their value. Other banks have treated these notes as part of their assets, so the failure of one bank causes the other banks to suddenly have fewer assets. Some of those banks may go under as well, eliminating the value of still more notes. The loss of value ripples outward; each bank failure reduces the solvency of other banks, and they fall like dominoes. To put it in psychological terms, when people lose trust in one institution, it causes other people to lose trust in other institutions, until everyone doubts the value of the money in their hands. Under such circumstances the smart thing to do is to convert that money into something tangible (land, gold, commodities) as rapidly as possible, which means getting rid of the bad money. This itself causes the money to lose value—it bids up the money prices of tangible things—giving people even more incentive to get shed of the stuff. It becomes a panic. Everyone is trying to shed paper notes, but the very act of doing so further devalues the paper and strengthens the incentive to get quit of it. The panic spreads until few or no money sources remain trustworthy. This dramatically reduces the amount of money in the system and results in real economic contraction.

Will such things happen with wildcat currencies? Yes. How bad will it be? It depends on how currency managers handle assets.

Without question, an old-style financial panic can and will start with wildcat currencies. We will have hundreds if not thousands or millions of currencies, each managed by a private company, through which people may buy and sell things. Private companies occasionally go under. With wildcat currencies we can expect a high failure rate: there will be many such currencies, and most of the people running them will not be especially experienced or able money managers. Moreover, those who run virtual currencies may have the incentive to debase them in order to gain a quick bit of extra purchasing power before the broader money system becomes aware that the currency is less valuable.

In the past, the failure of one source of money has rippled out and caused others to fail. The key question is what will happen when a private virtual currency disappears, as it surely will. How will this affect the health of other virtual currencies, private and state-backed?

The answer depends on the extent to which other financial concerns rely on virtual currencies as assets to back their operations. Recall that a bank fails when a depositor comes to the window and asks for his money, and there is none in the vault. The reason is usually that the bank has lent out too much of the money deposited to it. Jones deposits one hundred gold bars in 1st Bank and Trust. The bank lends one hundred gold bars to Smith; Jones comes the next day and asks for one bar back, and there are none to give him. End of bank. But if Smith has used his gold bars to set up a business, earned twenty bars' worth of paper notes from 2nd Bank and Trust, and deposited them in 1st Bank, Jones can be given some of this paper money, and 1st Bank does not fail. When 2nd Bank goes under, however, the paper money in 1st Bank's vault becomes worthless, and if Jones comes for his deposit that day, 1st Bank fails. A financial concern, like any other, fails whenever it cannot make payments on its obligations.

The failure of a virtual currency will cause other virtual currencies to fail if the companies that run the other currencies rely on that virtual currency in a significant way to make payments on their obligations. Especially vulnerable are companies that accept deposits or investments and then use them to make loans and investments in other companies. If companies use private virtual currencies as part of these transactions—using Amazon Coins, for instance, as a reserve against the lending of dollars—then the entire system is vulnerable to a virtual currency collapse.

At this point, it would be nice if we were able to say that, of course, no responsible financial firm would rely on as questionable an asset as a virtual currency run by a social media company. In 2007, one might have said that no responsible financial firm would rely on as questionable an asset as a mortgage where the borrower's claimed income is taken on blind faith. We have seen in the collapse of 2008 how the sociology of investment can drive even reasonable money managers to take excessive risks. There is no guarantee that future banks and financial institutions will properly assess the risk involved in holding assets in a wildcat currency.

There are two comforting thoughts. First, virtual currencies are not currently designed to be a source of lendable funds. While real-world financial institutions may endanger themselves by relying too heavily on wildcat currencies, the currency operators themselves seem culturally averse to using their assets as a source of financial capital. They don't lend them out. Even though the owners of virtual money are in fact financial operators, they focus their business entirely on facilitating transaction and exchange, and take no part in investments and loans. The wildcat currency sector itself is not risky in that sense. It only creates risks for outside firms that may come to rely on these currencies as a source of asset holdings.

The second (somewhat) comforting thought is that wildcat currencies as a source of asset holding for financial firms are no riskier than any number of odd financial products already in existence. It is doubtful, for example, that a wildcat currency is harder to assess for its reliability and long-run health than the mortgage-credit products that caused the 2008 downfall. Wildcat currency probably will not add to the overall risk of the financial sector; it will merely provide a new playground for speculations that are bound to occur anyway. The simple, obvious (though not easy) cure for this has nothing to do with wildcat currency: let 'em fail.

Speaking of failure, what will happen to virtual goods when a virtual currency collapses? If a virtual currency goes under because the system from which it was born goes out of business, what happens to the balances in the virtual world and the goods that people owned there? One could argue that my virtual turnips in a game world have some actual economic value, and when the world goes under, I have a right to compensation in terms of real-world money. The terms of service of virtual environments now make me sign away any such claim, but it will be interesting to see what happens as the scale of virtual holdings increases. We may begin to see a virtual goods insurance system.

Virtual goods insurance may also protect against radical changes in the virtual worlds we inhabit. Currently, the owners of a social media environment or game are dictators of that space. They decide everything important in the world. They may, as we have seen, make decisions that render a currency valueless. They may make goods and services obsolete, effectively gutting their value. This happens quite often in games; a new "patch" is released, and suddenly the equipment that people worked (played?) so hard to obtain is now all second-tier. Value has been destroyed. Should there be a recourse?

In the real world, deposits in failed banks are insured to some extent by governments. In the United States, we have the Federal Deposit Insurance Corporation. Perhaps one day there will be a Federal Virtual Value Insurance Corporation.

THE VIRTUAL IS UNSTABLE

Our trust in wildcat currencies is wrapped up in the trust we have in all virtual goods, and in the economy as a whole. All currencies, tangible or virtual, state or private, experience price inflation. Some expose their holders to significant financial risk. The emergence of wildcat currency will not bring anything particularly new; rather, the world will return to an earlier state in which there are many different currencies and economies, each with its own degree of reliability and value. Trust will be a product of prudence, and the trick, as always, will be to gauge the prudence of your economic partners and make deals, or not, accordingly.

7

HOW MONEY WILL EVOLVE

Virtual currencies are now a small-scale phenomenon. Their total contribution to overall wealth is on the order of a small country. This contribution has grown rapidly, but will it continue to do so? To one way of thinking, it would seem that most virtual currencies will go away. Money is subject to network effects, and network goods become more valuable as more people use them. This leads to a prediction that the biggest currencies will be the most valuable, and will therefore wipe out any competing, little currencies. Yet there is more to money than its network features. We see today a proliferation of little currencies even though we already have several massive, global currencies. To predict the future of money, we must go beyond network economics and think more broadly about the category of things to which currencies and economies belong.

INSTITUTIONS

There are any number of ways to generalize, but we will focus on the concept of *institutions.* First developed in political science, an institution is understood as the equilibrium of a social interaction.[1] An equilibrium is a situation in which each person's strategic choice makes good sense, given the strategic choices of everyone else.

Driving on the right side of the road is an example of an institution. The social interaction is driving, and the strategic possibilities are to drive on the right or on the left. Given that everyone else drives on the right, it makes good sense to drive on the right. Driving on the right is thus an equilibrium strategy in this situation. So is driving on the left: it makes good sense to drive on the left if everyone else does. An out-of-equilibrium choice would be to drive on the right when everyone else is driving on the left. Equilibria in social interactions are situations where the choices of the people in the situation are self-confirming. Each individual choice makes sense, given the pattern of choices across the whole group; and the pattern of choices across the group makes sense in that it emerges from the sensible decisions of each person.

There may be many different equilibria in a social situation, which is to say, many different sets of behaviors that all make sense together. Driving on the right makes sense if everyone is doing it; so does driving on the left. We can therefore speak of the *institution of driving on the right* as opposed to the *institution of driving on the left.*

In a similar vein, we can speak of the U.S. Constitution as an institution: it persists and is sustained by the mutually reinforcing choices of voters, the president, the Congress, and the Supreme Court. The Constitution as it stands today, however, is not the only such document that could be so sustained. Other constitutions might survive equally well. Each one is a particular institution, a particular equilibrium for the grand social game of national politics.

The institutional view of social phenomena stems from game theory, a field that emerged in the middle of the twentieth century from mathematics, political science, and economics. It is a general, abstract way to look at society and its changes. While it often focuses on incentives and prices as the source of change ("if you create laws against left-driving, you can switch a left-driving institution into a right-driving institution"), it need not. Another way to imagine change in social equilibria, in institutions, is to use concepts of evolution.

INSTITUTIONS AND EVOLUTION

The field of evolutionary game theory proposes that institutions may change due to evolutionary pressures. Survival and adaptation pressures affect not only living organisms but cultural entities.

Living organisms are subject to evolution because they have offspring whose characteristics change randomly, and they live in an environment that kills or disadvantages offspring with certain characteristics while allowing offspring with other characteristics to thrive. Entities in human culture, although they don't replicate the way organisms do, may have similar features.

Consider the abstract concept of *strategy*, understood as a choice made when certain informational conditions are present. An example of a strategy might be, "If my breath is bad, I brush my teeth." A strategy can be thought of as having offspring in the sense that it may be copied by other people, including our future selves. Children copy the toothbrushing strategy of their parents (usually unwillingly), but one's dental hygiene may also be adopted by a classmate, work partner, or roommate. Strategies pass from one time period to the next through cultural transmission. Like organisms, they are subject to selective destruction and growth. The world reacts to strategies, and it may react in a negative way. To see this, go without brushing your teeth for a few weeks. The social stigma you experience will probably make you change your mind, effectively "killing" that strategy. Not only will it be killed for you, but the same stigma will prevent others from adopting the strategy. Smelly green teeth as a hygienic strategy is like a mutation that kills its bearer. It will not survive in this particular jungle. In some human societies, the strategy of not brushing your teeth every day will survive. The survival of strategies is determined by their environment.[2]

Starting with this insight, the field of evolutionary game theory has built an elegant approach to social change.[3] In this theory, it is proposed that people maintain their strategies until they don't work well. Then they switch. Social change is the result of millions of individual strategy switches.

For example, a man might have a habit of holding doors for women. The strategy might work very well at one time; the ladies smile. But over time, let us suppose, the ladies begin to frown. The social encounters resulting from this strategy have turned negative. The man therefore changes his strategy. Perhaps he switches to "hold the door for everybody." Or he may change to "hold the door for nobody." Or he may try "hold the door for people wearing red." Whatever he tries next, he accumulates social payoffs and makes decisions, retaining strategies that produce smiles and dumping ones that don't. In this way, subtle changes in attitude get translated into changes in behavior.

The theory assumes that we don't reflect about our choices too often, which, on reflection, is a pretty good assumption. We have habits that we follow. When we get in the car, we drive on the right if we're American, on the left if we are Japanese. We don't think about it, we just do it. So does everyone else. Since we generally don't encounter people doing the opposite thing, we keep on with our habit and don't reflect on it. The man formed a habit of opening doors for ladies when he was young, and it might take many years of scowling before he realizes it is not appreciated as it once was.

Change accelerates when we encounter people who are already doing things another way. I may change my strategies because I get bad payoffs, but I may also change because I see other people getting better payoffs. People copy. Consider the example of fashions. In the world of fashion, it generally is good to judge what the rest of the world is doing and then make a choice that fits. But fashions change all the time, and if you do not change, in this game, you may end up being the loser. How do we keep up with fashion? Some people put a lot of thought into it. They read the magazines and watch the shows and carefully note what famous people are wearing and what seems to be hot. Most people, though, change in a less conscious way. They wear clothes in which they feel comfortable. And then, one day, those bell-bottom jeans with rhinestones just don't feel comfortable any more. When you wear them you feel "out of it." Or when your pants get worn out, you find it hard to replace them; stores don't carry them anymore. Or you see another person in slightly different type of pants and you think you might look pretty cool in those. You copy what she's wearing, you feel good about it, and your attitude shows. Other people wear the new pants too. You yourself wear them again and again, and the bell-bottoms gradually slide to the bottom of the dresser.

According to evolutionary game theory, the bell-bottoms were a victim of selection. They were no longer adaptive for the current state of the social jungle, so they died. They did not have offspring; no other person saw them and said, "Wow, those look great, I want to wear something like that." Instead, a mutation on the bell-bottoms proved to have more offspring, spawning many thoughts of "I want to wear those." Those moments when someone decides to make a fashion statement are the equivalent of a mutation in the social scheme. If the fashion statement succeeds, others copy and it grows. If it doesn't succeed, it dies off. The cool new pants thrived, the bell-bottoms went the way of the dinosaur.

The example shows how evolution explains social change. The fixed points of society are its institutions, and these institutions change as the choices of individuals respond to the current state of society. The changes can be slow or rapid. A wonderful example of rapid change happened in East Germany in 1989, when the institution of socialist government, which had been supported for years by the habits of the people, even though most of them felt there must be a better institution, suddenly collapsed when those people made a collective switch in their minds.[4] Gradual change in institutions happens in cases like the decline in childbearing in western Europe.

Year after year, fewer people have children. The thought "I want a big family" is not spreading as well as the thought "I do not want children." Society still fits together, but it is fitting together in different ways as a result of these changes of mind. For example, fewer western Europeans are getting married. It still makes sense for X percent of the population to be married, but X is a declining number.

If money is an institution, we can use this approach to predict how wildcat currencies will evolve and possibly change the institutions of the brick-and-mortar economy.

MONEY AS AN INSTITUTION

Is money a social institution that thrives or declines under evolutionary pressure? In Chapter 4 I described the concept of a coordination game, of which right- and left-side driving is a fine example. In coordination games, everyone does better if their choices all match.[5] Money is certainly the outcome of a coordination game: It makes sense to treat a form of money as having value if everyone else treats it as having value. If everyone else treats it as valueless, it makes sense for you to do the same. When we see a form of money being actively used in a population, we are seeing an institution in place. The specific form of money—the labeling of one commodity as "money"—is the result of an equilibrium of choices. Some actors' choices have more weight than others. The U.S. government's choices (to declare U.S. dollars to be legal tender; to use dollars for all of its finances; and to issue new dollars at a certain rate) certainly have a huge effect on the perceived value of the dollar. My point is that this is not all there is to the story. The equilibrium state of the value of dollars is affected by the choices of everyone—the government but also everyone else.[6]

What choices are these? One is the choice to treat a thing as money. Another is to judge an individual unit's purchasing power. We can imagine evolutionary change in both dimensions. For example, a thing that is money one day may not be money the next. When the U.S. Civil War ended, Confederate dollars changed from money to mere paper. Alternatively, the purchasing power of money may change gradually, as we have seen with inflation. Inflation is an interesting case of evolutionary game theory at work. When everyone else raises prices by 3 percent, it makes sense for me to raise my prices by 3 percent as well. It makes no sense in an inflating economy to keep your own prices fixed—you will get the same number of dollars from your sales, but they will be worth less. Given inflation, everyone should inflate. It is like driving on the right, a self-confirming strategy. An inflation rate can be seen as the result of a coordination game about how rapidly money is losing value.

This recalls one of the most important features of coordination games, the role of expectations. I argued in Chapter 6 that money can be brittle because its value is based on expectations about other people's behavior. An expectation is simply a mental state, and a mental state can change at any time, for any reason or no reason. Expectations can be affected by signals and history, as in the case of right-side driving. Even if you began the day driving on the left, all kinds of traffic signals and communications from others would urge you to switch. Moreover, given America's history of right-side driving, you are unlikely to consider left-driving in the first place.

Nobody wakes up and says "Hey, today I will try driving on the other side of the road for a change, see what happens." History and prior experience send us a signal: "Nobody else is doing it. Bad idea." In the arena of money, the signals are things like the statement on every U.S. dollar: "This note is legal tender," which is to say, "You are holding *money*, not just a piece of paper." The government's fiat power is potent. Its declaration turns mere paper into money not because policemen will chase down anyone who treats dollars like paper but because the declaration itself changes expectations about how the economy will treat dollars. History matters as well—if a commodity has been money for some time, its status as money will generally be assumed. Money has value so long as we expect it to have value. It is an equilibrium in a vast coordination game.

If so, then money meets the definition of an institution, and evolutionary game theory can help us understand how it will change. According to evolutionary game theory, institutional change happens when people change their strategies. Sometimes this is because they change their minds due to payoffs, but sometimes it happens because they observe other behaviors and switch. So long as humans reflect occasionally and observe one another, strategies may change, and institutions with them.

In the case of money, change happens when expectations about value change. In looking for signs of change in money, then, we should look for emergent histories and new signals that might change people's expectations about what money is and what it is for. I can imagine two ways this could happen, one gradual and the other abrupt.

GRADUAL CHANGE

Gradual change can be thought of as a cultural invasion. A new way of behaving spawns randomly somewhere, and then spreads like an infection. It starts with a few cells, but the bacteria reproduce more quickly than the body's cells can wipe them out. The infection grows until either the body manages to reverse the growth or the bacteria kill the body. In the same way, a few people may develop a new way of doing things and their behavior may cause others to do the same. If the rate of switching to the new behavior exceeds the rate at which people switch back from the new behavior to the old, then the behavior grows in the population. This continues until the new behavior either meets some check, such as being met by a counterbehavior, or completely dominates the population.

A good example of such a dynamic is the game rock-paper-scissors. Imagine a society of rock-paper-scissors players in which everyone always chooses the strategy "rock." Everyone ties, every time. Suppose one person chooses to change, and tries scissors. That person learns immediately that this is not a good idea—his scissors is broken by rock, and he loses. He goes back to rock. Suppose someone else chooses paper. This person succeeds—his paper covers rock, and instead of tying like everyone else, he wins. He, of course, tells others about it, and others see that he has won. They think, "I should try paper too!" And they do. Since most of the population is still playing rock, all of these switchers win their games, further propagating the idea that paper is a good strategy to play. Paper-playing rises in the population. As the proportion of those playing paper rises, it makes less sense to play rock. If 98 percent of the population is playing paper, rock is almost guaranteed to lose. Once paper becomes the new norm, a sensible person would switch from rock to paper, until everyone is playing paper. Thus paper can start as a tiny strategy innovated by one person, then grow to become the strategy that everyone plays. Of course, once paper dominates, a small innovation to scissors will grow. The eventual dominance of scissors leads back to rock. The system, in other words, can be cyclical.

The gradual invasion model is the best way to understand some of the most famous examples of monetary change in the past. Recall Gresham's Law: "Bad money drives out good." Gresham was commenting on the policies of Henry VIII, who had taken the English shillings in his possession, which were pure silver coins, and had their silver content reduced by 40 percent, replacing the silver with base metals. Henry's coins still said "One Shilling," but they no longer held one shilling of silver. They were "bad" money, money whose face value is less than the value of the commodity of which it is composed. Yet there was still "good" money in circulation, shillings that said "One Shilling of Silver" and actually *were* one shilling of silver. By law all merchants had to accept a shilling of any quality as a shilling. The shilling was a coin of the realm and had to be taken as payment. It was legal tender, just as our dollar bills are today. Under these circumstances, it behooved no one to use the good money to pay for anything. Say I have two coins, one pure silver and one half-silver. Each weighs two ounces. I can use either one to buy a cow. If I use the good coin, I gain a cow and lose two ounces of silver. If I use the bad coin, I gain a cow and lose one ounce of silver. Clearly it is best to use the bad money. If two forms of money are forced under law to have the same value in exchange, Gresham theorized, the one with less commodity value will become commonly used for trading, and the other will be removed from circulation. Bad money drives out good.

We are interested in the process by which this happens. Bad money drives out good in a slow, gradual, autonomous manner, through the choices of individual actors. The disappearance of pure silver coins in England in the sixteenth century was noticeable but gradual. Folks who had coins simply kept the good ones. The coins used in transactions came gradually to be the debased coins only. Individual decisions about which money to use resulted in a major change in the coinage used throughout England.

Today, if we use the terms the way Gresham's Law does, some wildcat currencies are good and others are bad. First, it should be noted that state-backed currencies today are all bad: they are all not only debased but debased 100 percent. All state currencies are fiat money, and fiat money has no commodity value whatsoever. There is no silver in the shiny coin, and nothing of value at all in the paper bill. For a long time, these tokens could be exchanged for tangible commodities, especially gold, so it might be said that they were "good money" in Gresham's sense. But all countries had abandoned the gold standard by 1971, leaving us in a world in which the official currencies are all completely "bad."

Some wildcat currencies look, by comparison, more like "good" money. Frequent flyer miles are an example. Supposedly, the airlines that issue FFMs stand ready to exchange them for a tangible service, a flight, at a fixed ratio. The FFM thus has a de facto commodity value.

There are also examples of quasi-good money. The currencies in the Facebook payments system can be exchanged with Facebook at the rate of seventy cents on the dollar. The currencies are backed by the dollar, apparently. But since the dollar is itself "bad" money, what does that make a Facebook currency?

Another example of quasi-good money comes from games. Game companies issue gold coins and then put merchants in the world that stand willing to accept any amount of these coins in return for virtual commodities. For example, a game I am currently playing allows me to take gold coins I pick up in the world and use them to buy boots for my avatar. I can buy an unlimited number of boots. Is it fair to say that my gold coins are "good" money, with a commodity value anchored in the utility of these boots? Boots are commodities, even if virtual ones—they provide a service to their owners. The rate of exchange between game currency and boots is fixed. It does not depend on market forces but is set by the company. It does occasionally change, but only through an explicit policy decision by the developers. Can virtual goods sold by game merchants be considered the backing of a currency?

In the game EVE Online, players may use coin collected in the world to purchase subscription time in the game. Is the virtual currency therefore a good currency, backed by the commodity value of a month's subscription to the same game?

Indeed there are few examples of completely "bad" nonstate virtual currencies, currencies that have no commodity value at all. (The Bitcoin is one of these rare examples.) The game companies that issue virtual gold coins do so with the express intent of allowing players to trade them with the company for virtual commodities.

The only truly bad virtual currencies are state-backed ones; only the state promises nothing in return for the money it issues.[7]

By Gresham's Law, then, if there were a fixed rate of exchange between "bad" money like dollars and "good" money like FFMs and gold coins, we would see the dollar replace the virtual currencies almost completely. People would hoard the virtual currencies and trade only with the "bad" dollars.

There have already been examples of this kind of phenomenon. In many online games, it is common for third-party commercial companies to offer to "power-level" a player's character. The player gives his account information to the company, and the company, for a fee, hires workers to play the game and take the character from Level 1 all the way to Level 50 or whatever is the top level. Then the character is returned to the player. The fee is usually demanded in dollars (or yen or euros), not the money of the game. This may happen because players interested in power-leveling also may not have much game currency; or because real-world monies can be used to buy so many more things. On the other hand, games where power-leveling is frequent also commonly have players exchanging the game currencies for state-backed currencies on shadow markets. In other words, the game currency is completely liquid and can easily be transferred into dollars or whatever real-world currency is desired. Moreover, the people hired by the company to do the power-leveling are of course players of the game—you might think they would enjoy being paid in terms of the game currency, since it obviously can buy things that they want. Yet power-leveling companies operate entirely on the basis of real-money payments. It leads one to wonder whether the "badness" of real-world currency is also part of the reason. The game currency is backed by the goods of the game. It is "good money" in the sense that you can always exchange it for commodities at a fixed and unchanging rate. Yet this market prefers to use dollars.

There is other evidence of a preference for "bad" money in the virtual economy. Blizzard Entertainment's Diablo III enables players to trade virtual goods through an Auction House. This is common. What is uncommon is that Blizzard allows the traders to use dollars, euros, and yen in a special Real Money Auction House. There is a game currency, the gold coin, that can be used in the game to buy things. But here we have a choice by developers and players to trade with a bad currency instead of a good one. As above, the issue is confused by the infinitely wider scope of the real-money economy and the much greater purchasing convenience of dollars as opposed to game currency. Yet game currencies are easily converted to dollars on third-party markets. Why, then, bring the dollar into the game, if not because bad money drives out good? The ultimate success of the Real Money Auction House model depends on the strategic decisions of millions of individual players. If it is to grow, it will grow gradually as players decide where to do their trading and in what currency. This is a microinvasion phenomenon, a gradual change from one money institution to another.

Games and social media offer many other examples of gradual monetary change. Game currencies can become completely debased through a design flaw, and then be gradually replaced through player action. This happened several times in the game Asheron's Call. The official game currency was the pyreal. Through an unfortunate design choice, it was quite easy for players to "grind" pyreals. "Grinding" is a practice of not really playing the game but simply focusing on the acquisition of a specific good. Players in grinding mode seek out the spots in the game world with the highest rate of acquisition of the desired object. Then they sit there and repeatedly do whatever it takes to get the resource, grinding away, reaping the object at the greatest possible rate. For example, suppose players realize that the treasure they receive from a certain dragon is 1 percent more valuable, without limit, for every Shard of Wisdom they happen to own. Players have an incentive to find out where they can get Shards of Wisdom and to acquire them in the most efficient way possible. If Shards of Wisdom are acquired only by doing the Monk's Quest in the valley of Shangri-La, you will find hordes of players crowding Shangri-La to do that quest over and over and over. This behavior is usually unintended by the developers. The Monk's Quest was probably designed as a one-off adventure. The Shard of Wisdom was given its treasure buff in the dragon encounter as an afterthought. By failing to cap the benefit of the Shard, the developers unwittingly created a system that infinitely rewards doing the Monk's Quest. And therefore you see players grinding it. They are not actually playing the Monk's Quest; they are just doing whatever it takes to stockpile Shards of Wisdom.

In Asheron's Call, pyreals could be used to buy things from the system as well as from other players. They were also incredibly easy to get via grinding. Find a monster spawn point, kill the monster, get the pyreals he was carrying, wait for another monster to spawn, repeat. This method is available in many games and social media environments, but in Asheron's Call, the faucet was open far too wide. Pyreals flooded the marketplace. If you saw an expensive item for sale, you spent an hour or two grinding pyreals and bought it.

Inflation inevitably followed: prices on the Auction House spiraled out of control. As they rose, the incentive to grind for money went up: you needed to grind pyreals to get enough money to pay these outrageous prices. Soon every player was doing a lot of grinding. Because grinding is boring, third-party companies began sending in professional grinders, also known as "gold farmers," to grind the pyreals and sell them to players for real money. With all the players grinding and professionals grinding as well, money flowed into the system like water over Niagara Falls.

The developers responded as real-world monetary authorities often do, with a currency reform. They introduced pyreal notes with huge denominations. But they didn't turn down the faucet. Soon, of course, the new notes became as valueless as the original pyreals.

As the prices of goods in terms of pyreals skyrocketed, it became more and more cumbersome to use them to conduct trade. Without any planning or input by the developers, a new currency emerged: the Sturdy Iron Key, or SIK. SIKs were needed by all players to unlock things in the world and were rarer than pyreals. They had attractive properties in terms of weight and divisibility. Trade began to be denominated in SIKs instead of the official currency. Unfortunately, the core design of Asheron's Call allowed pretty much any good to be ground with efficiency, so as soon as the SIK became the de facto currency, it began to be debased by a flood of grinding. The player base gradually moved to a new currency, the Scarab, and the story was repeated. The emergence and reemergence of new currencies is entirely a phenomenon of gradual cultural change. Someone decides to denominate trades using a new item, and that strategy takes off in the population until everyone is doing it.

ABRUPT CHANGE

Other times, institutions change overnight. For centuries, Swedes drove on the left. But being out of step with the rest of continental Europe was painful, and a national referendum was held in 1955. Left-driving won, 83 percent to 15 percent.[8] In 1963, however, the Swedish Parliament voted to switch to the right, and the country did so on September 3, 1967. The change required a massive public awareness campaign. There were 150 accidents with no deaths. Switching driving sides is an institutional change that cannot occur gradually. Anyone who "innovates" will have a car accident within minutes. Everyone must change at once, or no one should change at all.

These considerations affect monetary change when entire systems of money are in play. When Germany was unified in 1990, the old ostmark was abandoned overnight. Similarly, any time a new social media platform launches its currency, there is an abrupt change in the platform's money system. When Amazon launched the Amazon Coin, a new monetary system was created instantly.

Abrupt changes in money systems require everyone in society to change all at once. Revolutions have a similar dynamic. Pressure for change builds and builds, yet nobody does anything. Then all at once, something happens—a new policy, a signal, a coordinating shout—and everybody changes.

THE LIKELY FUTURE OF WILDCAT CURRENCIES

Which kind of change are we most likely to see in the case of virtual money? Are there signs of small-scale strategy invasions, or pressures for large-scale change?

There certainly are signs of gradual change. New forms of money are being invented and used on a small scale. Some of these currencies seem to perform well in their designed tasks and are being copied. We can see a clear line of evolutionary cultural transmission from Ultima Online's gold to World of Warcraft's gold to Facebook's credits to the Amazon Coin. Wildcat currencies do seem to represent a practice that can invade other domains.

At the same time, there seems to be some invasion in the other direction. As we saw with the Diablo III dollar-based Auction House, state-backed currencies are better for many purposes than designed boutique currencies. Perhaps their domain will expand; perhaps the dollar will acquire many of the useful features of boutique currencies, and thus invade virtual economies.

Other currencies are neither boutique nor state currencies. Bitcoin is not a niche currency and enjoys no state backing. Its advantage is its limited visibility. Will the obscurity of Bitcoin transactions encourage its gradual spread?

Which form of money should enjoy the most confidence today? Whom do we trust? In a world of uncertainty, choosing the silo in which to store one's purchasing power is a tough decision. Shifts in faith cause flight from one currency or asset into another. There is no reason to believe that virtual currencies will be immune to such flights. There may be many gradual shifts in the kinds of money people rely on.

The issue is not just confidence in the storing of money but also the earning and use of money. If you are to receive payment, how do you want it? Where will you buy what you need? People can socialize by chatting in the park, on the phone, or on Facebook. The economic values of parks, phones, and Facebook are all affected by these choices. So is the money. If a forum hosts vibrant human activity, its money will be valuable. If nobody goes there, its money will be worthless. If people continue to shift more time into the internet and away from brick-and-mortar interaction, wildcat currencies will gradually become more valuable, and real-world currencies will fade.

The profusion of many little currencies creates pressure to move value among them. In Facebook's case, this pressure spurred the creation of its behind-the-scenes digital value transfer system. We will probably go from having many small independent currencies to "ecosystems" of transferable currencies, and from there to global systems of virtual transfer.

So much for gradual change. Abrupt change is also possible. Here we look not for signs of small innovations and gradual copying but for building pressure. One such pressure point is the legal status of virtual goods. We currently have a wealth of dual-currency systems, where a virtual economy has an internal currency partnered with a currency that trades one-way against the dollar. It is a cumbersome and perhaps unsustainable arrangement, but it will probably remain common as long as there are legal and policy questions about what a virtual economy really is and how it is to be treated. It is fascinating that the Blizzard company chose to name its dollar-based auction house a Real Money Auction House, thus implying that the money in its game is not "real." Companies and individuals seem to be relying on subtle strategies and implicit signals, as if waiting to find out what the state really thinks about virtual economies. When the state makes up its mind, there may be rapid change in virtual money.

There will probably be a sudden change in many state and nonstate economies when the legal and policy status of virtual worlds is finally established.

Pressure also seems to be building to fully and completely virtualize the real-money economy. We see this pressure in the form of increasingly fluid payments systems, such as debit cards and the Square payments system. Cash is disappearing. For real money to become completely virtual, however, will require a major policy change. State money would suddenly be seen not as a commodity but as a virtual item or token that the state disburses as it will. This would be a major change in consciousness, and quite the revolution indeed.

WHAT ABOUT THE REAL-VIRTUAL BORDER?

Finally, we need to address the common belief that institutions originating in virtual environments will stay virtual. It is comforting to assume that there must be some natural or technical reason why institutions in virtual worlds will not or cannot influence anything beyond their bounds. A basketball game, after all, cannot influence daily life very much; there are all kinds of natural and technical reasons why the behaviors and emotions that happen on the court generally stay there. Events in virtual worlds are in games, too. If I have no fear that basketball institutions will invade my daily life, why should I worry that online game institutions will do so?

You should anticipate these changes primarily because online games and social media platforms are not at all like "games" in the familiar sense. Persistent interactive social media are social worlds.

They are little societies—sometimes big societies. Can institutions spread from one society to another? Absolutely. The theory of evolutionary change of institutions relies on the transmission of strategies from one person to another. As long as people communicate across boundaries, the boundaries don't really matter. A boundary like "real/virtual" has no effect on behavior.

Anyone interested in these phenomena must understand that there are no natural or technical boundaries between the virtual and the real. There is no important difference between gold pieces and dollars. Nor is there a natural or technical difference between a raiding group in an online game and a networked work group in a corporation. There are differences, of course; but they are social, involving conventions, objectives, understandings, and expectations. They are not imposed by anything in the natural world or any technological limit. Being social, the differences are entirely susceptible to change.

There is no boundary that would stop the practices of a virtual economy from invading or altering those of the real economy. There is no sense in which the economic patterns that occur in games, social media, and online markets will naturally be contained there. It would be foolish to assume that social media economies will not provide examples or statements that may change the behavior of brick-and-mortar economic actors. Institutional change happens because people can observe one another and communicate about their experiences. Game and social media economies are eminently observable, and people in these environments communicate about their experiences, and not only within tiny circles of friends. Every person who is "in" a game economy or a social media economy is also "in" the real economy. She needs only observe and communicate to herself to effect a change in economic behavior in the real world. There is no natural or technical boundary keeping these economies apart. Institutional change will happen, and nothing about its source being "virtual" or "onlinc" will stop it.

Institutions do change under pressure. We may not know exactly what changes are coming to the institution of money, but we can say this: sometimes change comes slowly, like snowfall, and sometimes it erupts, like a volcano.

8

WILDCAT CURRENCY AND THE STATE

What should governments do with virtual currencies? The current backlash against the euro shows that a single unified currency is not necessarily the best final state of human money systems. We are apparently entering an age in which many currencies will be collected into digital value transfer systems. That DVTs have emerged in a vague legal and regulatory environment has three kinds of implications for policy. First, wildcat currency will have an influence on the current obligations of the government, for example in the area of crime control. Second, wildcat currency will directly affect the ability of the government to perform its functions. And third, it opens new possibilities for government action.

VIRTUAL MONEY AND CURRENT POLICIES

Policymakers should be aware of virtual currencies and the likelihood that they will become important in several areas.

CRIME

One advantage of a simple currency system such as we now have is the government's ability to observe and to some extent control economic transactions. This power has had a significant impact on the state's ability to enforce the law. Many illegal acts leave a money trail, and the state has been able to use its power to observe transactions to track down illegal acts and successfully prosecute their perpetrators.

This power of observation may be greatly diminished in a world of wildcat currencies. In Chapter 5 we discussed the possibility of an arms race in which wildcat currencies spread in breadth and sophistication while state technologies of observation and control seek to keep up. It is hard to imagine the state winning this race completely, to the point that it ends forever people's ability to conduct trades invisible to it. At the same time, the vast majority of trade is likely to be observed eventually by the state (and anyone else) who wishes to observe it. Currencies operate best when lots and lots of people use them; anything used by many people will be easy to observe. From a purely technological standpoint, we now understand that online privacy is the exception, not the rule.[1] Everything can in principle be observed and recorded. If there is to be privacy, it will occur by convention, norm, and law, not because observation is technologically impossible. While it will always be possible to hide something temporarily, it will be increasingly difficult to keep anything hidden forever. But there will always be a gap between what is done and what is recorded.

In that gap lives crime. Perhaps the key part played by wildcat currencies is money-laundering, the transfer of ill-gotten gains into assets whose provenance suggests legitimate business and nothing more. The potential for virtual money-laundering has already received scholarly attention, and the first regulations in the United States are being issued as I write.[2] It is simply enough done—you blackmailed the murderous heiress and now have $20 million in sordid cash. The serial numbers on the bills are known to be from her accounts. What if she goes to the cops, and they decide to find you by looking for the money you got from her? Very well—use the bills to buy $20 million worth of credits from a social media system. Then you sell the credits to other users for $20 million. You do all this anonymously, of course, making sure to use a wildcat currency worthy of the name: new, untracked, likely to vanish in a month or so. At the end of the process, you have clean money and the district attorney cannot use your accounts to connect you to the heiress.

Other criminal uses of wildcat currency involve the transaction of illicit goods, such as drugs, pornography, and weapons. Truly wildcat currency that comes and goes in a flash leaves little trace behind: "Yes, sir, I did have an infusion of $3 million into my account, but it was from sales of gold coins of my favorite game—certainly not surface-to-air missiles."

Wildcat currency may also play a role in evading taxation and regulatory oversight, a less exciting usage than arms sales but ultimately perhaps more significant. The moving around of assets is a cat-and-mouse game that auditors and businessmen play all the time.

Wildcat currencies work to the advantage of the businesses in this game by offering more places to hide and more ways to dissimulate. At times, these maneuvers cross legal lines. Someday, perhaps soon, a CEO will wind up in jail for failing to accurately report the true value of a wildcat currency.

Fraud is yet another area where wildcat currency will play a role. Game currencies have already been the targets of significant frauds and cheats. They are interesting not for their magnitude or for being fundamentally different from real-world fraud but rather for the way that they reinforce the old wisdom that a fool and his money are soon parted.

WARFARE

I have already mentioned the use of wildcat currency to conduct sales of illicit materials such as weapons. It may also be a weapon itself in the broader conflicts over control of the internet. In the shadow economy where fly-by-night monies will thrive, it will probably become common to marshal and deploy force elements using wildcat currencies. If you are hoping to get a botnet—a network of hacked computers that can be ordered to disrupt other computers— to attack a country you currently hate, there is no better way to do it than by distributing payments of a virtual currency to the bot computers, which can then forward it anonymously to their owners. The more evanescent and untraceable the currency, the better. For a particularly nasty trick, you could wait until an enemy's assets are bound up in a wildcat currency and then undermine or destroy it using a hack. In the future as in the past, money will be a big part of war. Wildcat money will be no exception.

STATE PURCHASING POWER

I noted in Chapter 4 that the historical legal grounds for fiat currency—money that has value because the state says so—rested on the state's need of purchasing power in times of emergency. It had to be able to print currency and use it to buy things. This principle allows the state today to produce any amount of money it wishes and then require private actors to accept the money as a form of payment.

Nonstate actors may also produce any amount of money they wish. But they do not have the state's power to force others to accept their money at face value, or at all. In the long run, neither does the state. Printing money and forcing it on the economy ultimately inflates prices, and while the state may insist that its bills be accepted, it may not control the prices that must be paid unless it takes over the entire private economy. Thus there are limits on both private and state issuers of currency: the more currency they create, the less buying power any one unit may command.

By the same logic, the state cannot really control the rate of exchange between its virtual currency and the virtual currencies of private actors. The day may come when the private currency of a social media network or a bank credit card may be more trusted than a state-backed currency. A particularly irresponsible government, or one with an incompetent or corrupt monetary policy, may see its currency lose value relative to a private currency.

This would raise a difficult question: does the state, in light of its demand for purchasing power in an emergency, have a right to seize virtual money of private actors? Imagine a day when the state's virtual currency has lost so much value that it cannot afford essential services, including interest payments. Currently the state has limited power to gain purchasing power by seizing financial assets. Are virtual monies protected from such seizure?

REGULATING FINANCIAL SYSTEMS

We have seen that wildcat currencies are likely to become implicated in the health of the financial system as a whole. Debates rage as to the proper level and method of financial regulation. It is hard to envision a future, however, in which wildcat currencies escape regulation. To the extent that they become part of the asset base of financial firms, they will become subject to accounting and reporting standards. There may also be restrictions on the financial products that may be made from wildcat currencies.

Governments have already acted to restrict virtual currencies' growth. The QQ Coin from an online game in China, for example, was banned by the Chinese government because it had become too much like a normal currency.[3] Central banks have been given the legal obligation to ensure the stability and soundness of the nation's financial system. This may justify widespread intervention in virtual currencies.

DEVELOPMENT

Virtual markets have the potential to provide income for people in developing countries.[4] Wildcat currencies break down or simply evade the barriers that keep wealthy people in postindustrial countries from hiring people in the global south for small tasks. Even a small flow of labor demand from north to south could dramatically improve living conditions. Of course, some sort of online connectivity would have to be available, but the dramatic rise of smartphone use points in this direction.

WILDCAT CURRENCY AND THE ABILITY TO GOVERN

Beyond these separate financial issues, the emergence of wildcat currencies has a broader implication for the overall power of the state. In a world of virtual currencies, it may become difficult for governments to collect the revenues they need to function effectively. If wildcat currencies allow businesses to evade oversight and control, they can also enable tax evasion.

UNCONSCIOUS TAX EVASION

Tax payments today rely to a great extent on voluntary compliance. Certain actors are notified by the state that it is their obligation to see that a tax is paid. Employers collect income taxes; retail sales outlets collect sales taxes. Note that the state identifies tax payment points based on its own ability to observe and control. There are far fewer retail sales companies than people who make retail purchases; thus it is easier to collect the tax from the sellers. Sellers are notified that it is their job to collect the tax and remit it to the government, and by and large they do. Employers collect income tax from their employees, and the employees file tax returns in a generally voluntary way. One way we know that much tax collection is voluntary is by the simple fact that the rate of auditing by the government is rather low relative to the amount of money involved.[5] The odds of getting caught cheating are actually quite low. Nonetheless, people comply.

What if they did not comply? I am not suggesting that wildcat currency will turn everyone into tax cheats. But it will create trading opportunities in which it will not be apparent to either party that a tax payment is due. Some wildcat currencies will be traded on large open markets like eBay, where sellers generally understand that their sales must be reported as income. But other trades will be thought of (at least by the participants) as neighborly loans rather than formal economic dealings. If you trade a chainsaw for your neighbor's hedge trimmer, you have incurred a tax burden, reportable in the United States on Form 1099-B, Proceeds from Broker and Barter Exchange Transactions. You probably didn't know that, and the Internal Revenue Service is unlikely to question you about it. Revenue agents might, however, take note if you and your neighbor decided to exchange houses. More specifically, real estate agents will know, and any lawyers you have involved, and they will cover themselves by insisting that the transaction be properly reported to the government. Tax will be due.

At what scale are transactions in wildcat currency less like trading a chainsaw for a hedge trimmer and more like trading houses? The size of the transaction is, of course, one obvious marker. But the virtual economy could make hundreds of millions of little transactions, each of which is too small to notice and is never reported through the ignorance and apathy of the participants, yet which add up to serious levels of economic activity. If so, they will also represent serious losses of state revenue.

The point is that obscure virtual currencies might evade observation by the state not because some people try to keep their transactions hidden but simply because the huge number of currencies and their rapid coming and going might keep people from realizing that what they're doing is reportable. If you didn't tell me I have to pay a sales tax when I go to Hobby Lobby, I wouldn't pay it—not because I am a lawbreaker but because it would not occur to me that buying a plastic flower is something that creates a tax burden. In a similar way, we may come to the point where many of our economic transactions have no apparent tax burden, even though some government insists that they do.

THE GLOBAL BLACK MARKET

A second looming challenge (for good or ill) to state involvement in the economy is the fact that the internet is international. It is quite common for games and social media to have vast international clienteles. We have seen that courts in different countries arrive at different judgments about the status of virtual goods. Should one country adopt a tax treatment of virtual assets, that treatment must somehow be communicated to and enforced upon the users from that country, and no one else. One can imagine tax-free worlds in haven countries, and debates about how funds created in-world must be transferred out of world.

PEER-TO-PEER AND THE LACK OF ACCOUNTABILITY

The larger issue in the long run is that the state may have no one to talk to. Today, most games or social media applications have a central operator who runs things. The state can make itself felt by leaning on the central operator. It can bomb the servers or indict the people in charge. But what if there is no central operator? What if a virtual world and the virtual currency it spawns are self-managing entities that simply live on the internet, with no central coordination or control?

One way this could happen is through peer-to-peer services. A peer-to-peer virtual world might not be affected externally by any actor. The only way to alter such a network is by entering it and projecting power from within. Obviously, the amount of power one node in a network can project is much less than the power projected by a state that can switch off the servers.

Yet even systems that are not peer to peer no longer have "central servers" as such. Every system consists of and lives in a cloud of computing assets. The clouds all talk to one another. There is no physical central point where the state can send its officers. It can indeed send police to a server farm and even seize it or blow it up. But whatever was on the server farm exists elsewhere and no doubt is programmed to respond to physical resource loss, whether through police or hurricanes, to fly to ever further points of refuge. Like a man trying to catch a thousand cats in a small room, the state will always see the system underfoot, and yet when it grabs for something, it will come up with air.

While the state cannot stop the data flow, it can put pressure on owners of data. But what happens when owners decide to remove to other jurisdictions or otherwise evade state pressure? It is not clear at all that the state will have much recourse other than to enter the system itself—become one of the cats—and hope to be heard in that fashion.

Reviewing these trends, it is not clear that the state will continue to exercise the influence over economic transactions that it has now. A decline in the size of government may be in the cards.

VIRTUAL CURRENCIES WILL REQUIRE NEW POLICIES

As wildcat currencies expand their scope, governments will be called on to clarify the legal and regulatory environment. At the same time, these currencies may become an interesting new tool for pursuing economic and social objectives.

STATE OBLIGATIONS TOWARD VIRTUAL CREDITORS

In some circumstances, the state may become the manager of virtual goods and wildcat currencies in the service of the common good. It has been noted that the bankruptcy of a virtual world could make the state the governor of that world.[6] The assets are valuable only so long as the world continues to function. A bankruptcy court's job is to sustain the value of assets until the failed entity can be fully liquidated or reorganized. Sustaining the value of virtual assets means keeping the virtual world alive. In this sense, the state may become the provider of last resort for virtual world and social media management services. The alternative, simply pulling the plug on the servers when a virtual environment fails, may seem quite risky, given that it may lead to significant disruption elsewhere in the economy. Can a virtual world be too big to fail?

One precedent for the reorganization of failed virtual worlds has already been set. It has already happened that third parties, completely unaffiliated with the owners of a virtual environment, have set up parallel "rogue" servers, just for their own less fettered entertainment. On your own server, you can change the rules to some extent and play however you wish. If the main company goes down, the third-party servers can then be used to keep the world alive. Thus a commercial world may enter the public domain, not through government takeover but through takeover by its users.

DATA COLLECTION

As I noted earlier, privacy is no longer a technical matter; it must be created and sustained by law and custom. The collection and use of data will be as much an issue in wildcat currency environments as anywhere else.

But a much bigger, more important issue about data looms already, and that involves basic national accounting. Virtual economies have been around for many years, growing exponentially. Yet there is no effort to collect formal statistics about their size and growth. If there is an observation arms race between wildcat currencies and the state, the state is not even aware of it yet. The hare is around the bend and the tortoise still thinks the event is a cakewalk. It would be extremely valuable for central governments to include virtual economic data in their statistical reporting. We would see the first conflicts, and have the first critical discussions of policy, when the government asked the developers of a fantasy game for data on its players and their economic activity.

A story once made the rounds—probably apocryphal—that the Internal Revenue Service had aspirations of collecting sales tax at the Burning Man Festival. Burning Man is an annual mass event that calls forth the oddball segments of American society in all their freakish glory. For a week it creates a city of thirty thousand people out in the desert, where there is much trading, none of it in dollars. Under the law, every trade of beads for henna incurs a barter tax obligation. The IRS is said to have sent an agent to investigate. He wandered in the madness for a few hours, until it became obvious that there would be no collection of barter taxes at Burning Man. It is simply too weird. For the same reason, it would be hard for a government to demand full revenue and regulatory reporting from the makers of virtual environments.

Nonetheless, it will become increasingly important to know how much value is being created and traded. Much of what occurs in virtual environments counts as subsistence production, meaning that a person makes something he uses himself and never trades. Should this be considered part of some nation's gross domestic product? What about things that are made and then sold to a robotic merchant system rather than to other players—is this production? What is value under these circumstances? The answers are often not difficult, but the sooner they can be found, the better the ensuing policy debates will be.

GOVERNANCE

Finally, it seems likely that the state will become embroiled in basic questions of political economy in the management and governance of virtual environments. Currently, users of these environments surrender almost every significant civil right in order to use the environment. Through the terms of service and end-user licensing agreement, users waive their rights to speak, assemble, worship, and own property. Surely this cannot stand, and a significant legal literature has already addressed possible remedies and sensible interpretations.[7] The issues around how virtual worlds should be governed are probably similar to those involving the governance of corporations, clubs, and sporting associations. Those who create and manage such entities are allowed to do so under certain constraints, and in the case of virtual environments, those constraints have yet to be determined.

USING VIRTUAL WORLDS TO TEST POLICY

Having observed virtual economies for some time, I believe they could be useful research and testing tools under controlled conditions. As virtual economies become much more like the real economy and vice versa, the conditions inside virtual economies have more and more relevance to conditions outside. But virtual economies are easier to handle. You can create exact copies of a virtual world and impose two different policies in them. The results will give you something rare in macroscale social science: direct evidence of causation.

Virtual worlds also give us direct information on the kind of economy that people want. Suppose we were to set up many parallel virtual economies, each with slightly different policies. Suppose then we found that certain of these economies were quite popular with players, while others were less popular. This information would certainly have policy relevance. After all, shouldn't we build real-world policies that create economic worlds that people enjoy? The point is not as far-fetched as it may seem. Players in virtual economies are also citizens in real-world countries. Presumably, they vote for policies they prefer. We should not be surprised if voters clamor for policies in the real world that match policies they have enjoyed in their virtual worlds.

Moreover, all of society benefits when people choose to participate openly and eagerly in the economy. Economic participation is a concrete aspect of basic citizenship. People who willingly enter the aboveboard economy are expressing a vote of confidence in that economy. They must have some sense that their efforts will be rewarded fairly, that there is some scope for free choice, and that their own efforts to thrive are making the rest of the world a better place. If a virtual economy discovers ways to make these things happen, its policies very much deserve attention of real-world decision makers.

On a broader level, game designers and real-world policymakers face the same conceptual problem: they are expected to understand the interests of the populace and then create institutions that serve those interests. In the real world case, we call those institutions policy. In games, we call them rules. Game designers have additional power to use the game's code to make certain behaviors impossible, but game designers and policymakers are both constrained by human psychology. Both policymaking and rulemaking are examples of governance. If game designers and politicians are doing similar things, they can learn from each other.

Real-world governors may be interested to learn, for example, that game governors *always* test their policies before implementation. When I was in graduate school, policy testing was almost unheard-of in the real world.[8] Thankfully, a new era of testing seems to have arrived, with social scientists going into the field to study how controlled changes in policies affect individual behavior.[9] But a society is a huge, complex, dynamic system, and predicting the actual effects of policies (as opposed to individual behavior) is extremely difficult. Yet important, given the money governments spend. Nonetheless, no government of which I am aware maintains a systematic policy testing apparatus. As a result, policymaking in the real world is done poorly.

This is not to blame governments. There has always been an unbridgeable methodological gulf between the study of natural forces and the study of human affairs. In the former, it has generally been possible to conduct controlled tests of ideas. In human affairs it has generally been impossible to test anything even moderately complex. We cannot create two identical versions of Athens, impose Plato's Republic in one but not the other, and measure the resulting differences in eudaimonia. Today, however, game designers do this all the time.

HOW GAME DESIGNERS DO POLICY

The makers of games and social media systems have evolved ongoing design protocols that are like an assembly line for public policy. Massive online games are not just software but software-mediated service systems. They are always on. Each such system has a "live team" that constantly monitors the current state of the game. The live team implements tweaks and changes, called patches, as deemed necessary by the ultimate governors of the game, the top-level designers. Usually they are concerned about player happiness and its effect on revenues, but at times changes are necessary due to a technology breakdown or a hack. Such things are identified by automated tracking systems that highlight rapid change or anomalies. Online systems like this involve the real-time monitoring of millions of actions, by millions of people.

At the same time, each system has long-run development teams in the background, studying the data and thinking of ways to improve the user experience. What new content and features can be added? How can the service be made more attractive? Are there more fundamental problems that cannot be addressed by a patch and might require a more extensive redesign? Both the live team and the development team conceive of new things for the game or social media product, albeit on different time scales, short and long. As the new rules, content, code, and features are being created, the developers face the same problems that governments do. What should we be doing? What actions will best meet our overall goals?

For both governments and social media developers, the question "what should we be doing" has both idealistic and cynical answers. The cynical answers are "make money" and "get reelected." Both distill down into a common goal: "Get people to buy into what we are doing and support us." But this slides fairly easily into the idealistic answer for both, which is "Give the people good things." Setting aside the obvious opportunities for manipulation, coercion, and fraud, the job for both game developers and governments is the same: find out peoples' interests, and deliver on them.

Social media development teams, like governments, are in the business of figuring out how people are experiencing their systems, and reacting appropriately. Do people like what they are getting? Who is having problems, and what kind? What can we do to help? Even where there are no reported problems, are there opportunities for making things better? These questions are directed toward making people happier with the game, or social media product, or party, or state. Happy people will support those running the show.

Here's an example of how these concerns play out in the practical context of a game. A game is launched and does well for a number of years. Over time, however, the community management people, who monitor player opinion in game forums, email, and the press, report a generally growing unhappiness among a certain class of players, the "cloth casters." Cloth casters are wizards and mages of various sorts, who cast spells to protect themselves and attack enemies. These players—whose avatars can wear only robes, thus the name—are unhappy with their experience in player-vs.-player combat. They have complained to the community management team about being killed by rogues. Rogues, it turns out, have a power called "stealth" that allows them to sneak up on the casters and attack suddenly, without warning. The casters say they are not able to cast their defensive spells in time, and are thus vulnerable to stealthing rogues. Many report that they are leaving the game.

The analytics team for the game is asked to investigate, and it reports that indeed, the rate of subscription cancellation is highest among characters of the classes Wizard, Mage, and Conjurer in the five minutes immediately following a player-vs.-player contest. The team also reports a trend over the previous twelve months in which the number of players who make rogue characters has been rising. A year ago, 11 percent of the player population consisted of rogues.

Now it is 21 percent. Meanwhile, the proportion of cloth casters has fallen from 15 percent to 9 percent.

At the same time, the live team that monitors the actual gameplay every day reports that something might be wrong with one of the cloth casters' spells. Some players have opened customer service tickets complaining that the Shield of Defense spell is not working properly. It is supposed to go off instantly when cast, but in practice seems to take 1.5 seconds to take effect. This delay might explain rogues' success—if it is a true bug.

The development team reviews the data and concludes that the long-run health of the game will be damaged if it becomes perceived as "rogues-only." The current problem may be caused by a Shield of Defense bug. Therefore, the live team is told to reexamine the code of Shield of Defense and tweak it if necessary. If a bug is found, a fix should be rolled out in the next patch.

Meanwhile, the development team has to consider what to do if it turns out that there is no Shield of Defense bug or that the bug, once squished, has no effect on player complaints. The team can enhance the defensive ability of cloth casters, or it can decrease the power of stealthed rogues. The team goes about considering ways that cloth casters can possibly respond to sneak attack. Do players have the defenses they need? Are we making those defenses too hard to use or understand? At the same time, the development team also considers the powers of rogues. Maybe the stealth power should wear off when someone gets within ten feet of an enemy. Maybe it should work only in the shade.

All of these considerations, plus bug fixes, become part of the policy pipeline for the game. And this pipeline becomes the source for the game's ongoing policy evolution.

HOW TO TEST PUBLIC POLICIES

So far, this process is not completely unlike real-world policymaking. At this point, however, just before implementation, the two protocols of governance diverge dramatically. The main difference is in testing—precisely the activity that real-world social studies has historically found so difficult. Game and social media companies develop a policy pipeline, but then they test those policies. Only after passing a series of tests does a new system go live.

For instance, game developers often use a "test server." A replica of the entire system is created and then walled off. Either users are specially selected for the test server, or the server is made open to all. Users are told that the test server does not represent the normal game experience, that achievements there will not transfer elsewhere, and that the things they do or make or grow may be wiped out at any time. The test server, in other words, is not a place to "live." Yet it often allows players to jump over hours and hours of content gates to get to the good stuff right away, for free. If a proposed change involves a level–80 dungeon, it makes no sense to open the test server for only level–1 characters. Instead, everyone who makes a character on the test server begins at level 80.

The results from the test server are then used to roll out minor and major design changes. Every patch to a system, large or small, generally spends time—at least a week, and sometimes a few months—on the test server before going live. The goal is to prevent nasty surprises and to make sure that the proposed changes do not harm other parts of what is, after all, an incredibly complex system. Game developers assume that no amount of theorizing and conjecture can account for all possibilities. War strategists know that the first casualty of any battle is the plan. Game developers know that the statement "nothing can go wrong" is always wrong. Therefore they test as much as possible.

They also go slowly, and match their testing to the size of the changes being envisioned. Big changes are tested and tweaked for a long time. Revolutions, and policy "experiments" conducted on the live population, are guaranteed to bring bankruptcy. In general, careful attention is paid to the satisfaction of the governed.

A second form of testing is the "A-B test." Two designs of a game are proposed, version A and version B. Version A is live on the service. Version B is then given to some subsample of new users, without their knowledge. A person signs in and tries out the game and, unbeknownst to him, gets version B of the game instead of version A. Like anyone else, this new user plays the game and decides whether to come back, or even whether to pay. The developers watch these numbers carefully. If version B gets more users to stay and pay, it must be doing something right. If that experience is confirmed in further tests, version B becomes the default game for all new users. By conducting successive A-B tests, the developers can gradually refine game systems. Over time, the game gradually changes, always moving in the direction of engaging more people for longer.

WHY GAME TESTING IS BETTER THAN REAL-WORLD POLICYMAKING

Let's contrast game testing with real-world policymaking. Game and social media testing regimes put the user—the citizen—in the center. Policies go into effect only if they will improve users' satisfaction with the game. Although game changes admittedly make some people angry, the game development process is aimed not at the edges of the populace but at its core. A policy change takes effect if it seems to make the game better for a vast majority of the people. If only that could be said of real-world policymaking!

Game policy development is based on how players react to proposed changes *before* they go into effect more generally. It is not based on conjectures and predictions, still less on arguments over style and ideology. Users don't have to guess what the effects of a change will be; they can go try them out. Discussion thus proceeds on the basis of concrete experience rather than guesswork.

Real-world policymaking, by contrast, tends to be dominated by narrow interests, is developed haphazardly in a process of deal making, is based on theoretical or ideological concerns, and has effects that are generally unknown or poorly predicted at the time the policy is issued.

There are several advantages to the game method. First, it is slow and incremental. Policy uncertainty imposes huge burdens on an economy. People in all walks of life must take into account the possibility that a government policy may change significantly. This causes hesitation and expenditures to hedge against risk. It is therefore better for policy to move slowly and predictably. An economy given time to adjust to a change will do so in the most efficient manner. This is better than policy revolutions.

Second, the game method of doing policy is based on genuine behavioral reactions. Votes, like surveys, are just expressions of desires. There's no reality check with a vote; it costs nothing to vote one way or another. Behavioral change is costly. We can reliably say that if people change their behavior in response to a policy, the effect is genuinely related to their well-being and their conscious or unconscious decision making. The game method therefore puts the citizens, their welfare, and their decisions in the center of policy-making.

COULD GAME GOVERNANCE METHODS WORK IN THE REAL WORLD?

Throughout this book, we have wrestled with the idea of *transfer:* do things in the virtual world transfer into the real world? Transfer is increasingly important in many fields that are concerned with virtual worlds and games. In education, for example, many people are interested in the way lessons learned in games transfer to real life, and whether that transfer is better than that offered by classroom teaching. This book has been largely about the transfer of virtual economic institutions into real economic institutions. The bottom line is that transfer happens, sometimes, but the road from virtual to real is crooked.

How might governance transfer from virtual to real? This has partly to do with the virtual world, and partly to do with changes in the real world. We have seen that technology has changed the real economy so that currencies once found only in games are now everywhere. Technology is changing the policy environment in similar ways. In a game world, the developers sit in their offices and proclaim rules via forums, blogs, and in-game messages. Players might hear about the policies from these sources, or from contacts who are also in the game. Governments, meanwhile, increasingly proclaim their policies via forums, blogs, and messages to "the world," meaning government employees, journalists, and government websites. Citizens might learn about the new policies there, or through emails and texts. The two systems are similar: decision makers sitting in a node on a vast information network, sending out rulings digitally. How long before the primary contact between the state and the citizens is direct email (or its successor)? "You are receiving this message because our records indicate that you are a citizen of the United States employed in automobile production. We are writing to inform you of a change in the Social Security treatment of automobile production wages. Please see hhs.gov/newsocialsecurity@rwages for more information."

At some point, the real world of governance will hardly differ in its communication technology from a virtual world. Then the introduction of game policy testing systems will be seamless. Moreover, the results of game-based policy testing could be used right now. There is no reason to stand by waiting for this beneficial tool to press itself into our hands. We could take it up immediately, and learn how to do policy iteratively, incrementally, and with a great deal of prior information about likely effects—a much better way to run a society.

FAUCETS AND SINKS FOR THE REAL WORLD

The confluence of virtual world technologies and the real-world economy may foster other innovations in public policy. Consider, for example, how game designers and real-world policymakers differ in their treatment of money. Government actors see money as a core property of the economy they have inherited from the previous government. They cannot imagine money as something separate from the banking system. Game designers, by contrast, see money as something they have created. For them, "managing" money has a different meaning: to manage money is to design trades and markets so that players enjoy what they are doing. In games and social media environments, the goal of monetary policy is to make people happy, and thus to keep them in the game.

What if real-world money managers had the same attitude? We know, for example, that people like to have money. In the real world, you get money only by working for someone else, by selling something, or as a payout from the state. In virtual worlds, you can get money almost on demand. Kill a monster, get a coin. Killing the monster is completely meaningless in economic terms. The act itself adds no good or service to the game world's economy. It produces nothing that can be bought, sold, saved, and used later. It's like shooting a basketball at the basket—something a person does just to do it. The game makes a person feel even better by adding a little money reward on top of the fun of killing the monster. People love little money rewards, and so game and social media systems give the user money for doing all kinds of little things in the system. Money is given out, in other words, for purely hedonic reasons.

Imagine a real world in which every time you sank a basket, the government gave you a penny. Every day you commuted to work, the government gave you $1. Or every day you exercised, you got $5. What if this was the way that the government injected money into our world—not as the result of reserve lending or bank notes or stamped coins, but as pure fiat money given away to make people happy? Then, like game designers, the government would have to invent "sinks," ways to remove money from the economy so as to keep its value stable. One easy sink would be to take tax money and simply destroy it. There's really no reason why real-world governments could not operate on a faucet-and-sink system just as game economies do. Or, like game economies, the real economy could have multiple currencies that do different things.

The reason this has happened in virtual worlds is simple. Game and social media operators have learned that the direct disbursal of money is an incredibly powerful way to make people happy while they are running about doing things. This system is combined with an experience point system so that people who do things in the game not only get more money but gain powers. Such methods can induce people to commit quite a lot of time to activities that one would not normally view as "fun." For example, the grinding activity we saw in the previous chapter is not fun, yet people do it in order to have more fun later. We have seen in games that you can get people to do work in return for promised rewards of money and power. The difference is that the way people get money and power in a game is designed to maximize their overall happiness.

The state could encourage all kinds of desirable behavior in this way. Driving properly, staying out of jail, staying in school, not having kids out of wedlock, exercising, paying taxes on time—all of these things could be rewarded with small direct payments, not out of a government budget but simply as a function of government fiat.

Would this pump lots of money into the system? Of course, but this need not lead to runaway inflation. Game and social media operators have learned how to manage their money supplies. When they introduce a faucet, they also open up the sinks. The government already has access to sinks; it would simply need to use them.

Such a system would probably pump most of the money in at the bottom of the income distribution, where it produces the most happiness. A dollar a day for staying in school doesn't do much for the children of a CEO, but it may make a difference for someone living on the streets. It is worth noting as well that game economies contain very little envy. The route to making money is open to all, and hence the accumulation of vast wealth by some players is received calmly by poorer players. Most seem to understand that they could have had, indeed still could have, that much money if they wished to put more time and effort into it.

If the concern is that we would be paying people to do things they should do anyway, consider this—game and social media systems often give people money for doing nothing at all. What if everyone got $5 per day simply for being human? It's not as far-fetched as you might think. Many countries offer basic income guarantees. Is there any difference between a minimum income guarantee and a general dispersal of fiat money in exchange for meaningless tasks?

Obviously these policies implicate the national debt. Or do they? Right now we force the government to operate on a cash-flow basis—what it spends must be collected through fees, taxes, or borrowing. But why? The "governments" of social media systems simply issue money when more money would help their world and destroy it when there is too much. They operate under no budget constraint whatsoever. Why not let the real government do the same? If the world needs dollars, let the government print dollars and spend them. If the world has too many dollars, let the government tax activities and throw the money away.

These ideas should not be taken as immediate policy suggestions. It is simply illuminating to reflect on the ideas that begin to flow when one approaches real-world monetary affairs using the policies of virtual economies. One encounters many notions that seem rather mad at first but then lead one to ask, "Why not?" The economies of games and social media seem to function well—look at the many millions of users and the rapidly growing aggregate value of their economic output. These money management methods might be radical, but they seem to work. Faucet-and-sink money for the real world—why not?

REQUIREMENTS AND CHALLENGES FOR GOVERNANCE

The state has explicit duties and severe challenges in the era of virtual economies and wildcat currency. It must maintain monetary order and stability in what apparently will be a rather wild time in monetary affairs. It must let games be games, and in fact should help games stay games and not blend in with the real world. At the same time, the state must establish a level playing field between social media networks and brick-and-mortar economic entities; there's no economic reason, certainly, for laws to differ across the digital divide unless the state explicitly desires to subsidize and encourage the development of social media systems.

The challenge for the state is heavy. It must continue its core functions in a world whose economy is fast slipping into the virtual and putting the continued feasibility of many policies in question. At the same time, there will be many examples of governance in virtual spaces that seem to provide reasons for dramatically changing what the state does and how it operates. All of this predicts severe disruption for the governments of the real world.

The lines between the real and the virtual continue to blur. It is not a case of the fantastic becoming more real or the real becoming more fantastic. Perhaps we are simply experiencing what happens when technology renders all imagination concrete.

EPILOGUE
DEAR POLITICIANS:
PLEASE DON'T SCREW THIS UP

Very soon, judges, legislators, and executives will begin to construct the legal and policy edifice that will regulate the relationship between virtual environments and the "real world" for generations to come. How they create virtual world law will determine much of our social structure in the digital age. It will be easy to do a terrible job; virtual worlds activate many conflicting thoughts, and we are built to become very angry over violations of the line between play and serious. The combination of confused thinking and strong emotion increases the chance that the authorities will mess things up. Even now, we are not starting out in the right way.

For example, we are building our online communities using contracts between individuals and companies. In this setup, no person has a legal relationship to any other person in the community. If a member hurts our online community, we have no social claim against him; our claims are treated as separate individual claims, not against the offending fellow but against the company. Any online village now exists as a group of people who share a contract only with a distant overlord, not with one another. That overlord generally expressly prohibits us from making legally binding agreements among ourselves. This arrangement chills the communal sense to the very bone, yet we take it for granted as the "normal" way to do virtual communities.[1]

There are many other things to worry about, but in this epilogue, I would like to underline what I believe is the single most important point. If policymakers ignore it, virtual worlds will develop in a very bad way.

Here's the point: when regulating or writing law for a virtual world, the goal of the virtual environment matters. Some virtual worlds are built for playing. Others are built for serious purposes. The law should treat them with equal respect, but differently.

A quick example clarifies the principle. Suppose Joe is a player in a fantasy game. He asks another player, Adam, to make him a piece of mithril armor. Adam does so. Adam gives Joe the armor, and Joe gives Adam one hundred gold pieces. Now suppose Adam is twelve years old and Joe is thirty-seven. Has Joe violated child labor laws? If not, why not?

Consider another example. This time, Joe has a Facebook app to promote his web design business. He asks Adam to visit the app at least ten times a day, and to write many positive comments about the business on Facebook's forums and commenting sites. He asks Adam to "like" the app and get his friends to do the same. In return, Joe tells Adam he can spend one thousand points on the American Express rewards site. Joe can do this because he is a longtime American Express user and has thousands of reward points with the company. Adam browses the American Express site and decides he would like a YoVille e-Game card, worth one thousand Amex points.[2] He tells Joe his selection, and Joe purchases the e-Game card using his points and sends the code to Adam, who uses it in YoVille. Now, does this arrangement violate child labor laws? If so, why?

I submit that the significant difference here is the purpose of the virtual environment where Joe and Adam are conducting their transactions. Facebook and American Express are serious companies doing serious business. So is Joe's web design company. The second set of transactions thus takes place in a context that is not remotely like a game. It is a business context. All the usual real-world laws should apply. Joe is hiring child labor. The first set of transactions, however, happens entirely within a fantasy game environment. It is not intended to be serious, and real-world laws should not apply. Joe is not hiring child labor, he is playing a game with a kid.

What would happen if the government were to ignore this difference, and treat these two transactions as being essentially the same? The result would be very bad.

If the government treated both events like a game, then Joe could evade child labor laws by conducting his business using American Express Rewards Points. This is completely unfair. It means that the laws of the land will apply differently to different businesses, depending on whether the owners have access to virtual currencies. If you use dollars in your business, you incur the whole weight of the governmental regulatory and tax burden. If you don't, you are free of the entire burden. Economists generally agree that if there is to be a regulation or a tax, it should apply equally to all similar businesses; otherwise you create incentives for businesses to change their behavior in order to exploit arbitrary loopholes. This is worse than unfair, it is inefficient. We want businesses to pursue value creation, not tax evasion. By treating everything virtual as if it were a silly game, government would create perverse incentives for all businesses to virtualize their operations.

What if the government errs in the other direction, and treats all virtual transactions as if they were serious? This also would be a terrible mistake, but for a different reason. If all state laws, taxes, and regulations were to land on every virtual transaction, no matter where it occurred, the entire industry of online games would be destroyed. Imagine you had to pay a sales tax every time you spent a gold crown to buy a Wizard's Pointy Hat. This would not only needlessly drag down the economy of these games, it would break their fantasy immersion. Without immersion in fantasy, the games are not worth playing. Without fantasy, online games are like basketball without a basket. What's the point?

The clear dividing line between fantasy games and serious social media can be drawn along the differences in purpose. The purpose of a fantasy game is to immerse people in fantasies and help them have fun. The purpose of serious social media is to help people connect, gain information, and conduct transactions. The latter is an ordinary function in the economy. The former succeeds only if it is *not* an ordinary function of the economy. Economies in online fantasy worlds are not business as usual. The government needs to treat them differently.

How can we best identify the line between serious social media and games? It is tempting to think about size; surely, games are small and serious social media are large. The problem is that in a wildcat currency environment, some game economies may grow very large indeed, and some social media economies may be very small. A collection of millions of small social media economies may have a greater collective impact than the official economies of entire countries. Thus it is important to discuss these issues in terms of type of economy and its goal, not just its size.

The proper distinctions may seem subtle, but I believe they are easy to apply in practice. Facebook is clearly a social media system. It is not a game. It hosts games, but it hosts other activities as well. Tera Online, on the other hand, is clearly a game. Though you can meet people in the game and trade things with them, it is expressly against the terms of service to use the system and its tools to promote or sell any good or service not attached to the game. You are even forbidden by the contract to use the real world to exchange game items.

The question that should guide policy is, *What is it for?*

In these two cases, this question is very easy to answer. Facebook is for connection, information, and business. Tera Online is for fun. If an environment is built to enable connection, it is a serious social media service. If it is built for fun, it is a game. Right now, this basically exhausts the universe of virtual environments, but if one should be launched that is for some purpose no one has seen before, the relevant way to identify that new type of virtual environment is by that purpose.[3]

In closing, I would like to address a powerful counterargument often given by the serious professionals in this area. Why protect games? Why should game economies be relieved of all these regulatory and legal burdens, while serious business must bear them?

First, we should be clear what is at stake. To impose any real-world burden on a game is to destroy it. It is in the nature of games that they do not touch reality. When reality enters a game, it ceases to be a game. We confront this fact whenever an athlete is seriously injured in a game: play stops and, for all players and all but the most callous fans, treating the injury and getting the player safely off the field takes immediate precedence. Football players who tackle opposing runners and baseball pitchers who hit opposing batters are not charged with assault and battery. Games do not tolerate contact with reality. They are extremely brittle in this regard.

We owe the idea of play space, where the rules are different, to the first dedicated theorist of play, Johann Huizenga.[4] His core concept was the "magic circle." The rules inside the magic circle of play are different. If we do not protect the magic circle, the rules of daily life invade the play area and destroy the play going on inside it. The magic circle is not a natural thing. It exists because we establish it and declare, "Anyone inside this space should act according to the rules of the game being played here." The magic circle, since it is not a natural boundary but an artificial one, cannot oppose or resist anything on its own. We create play when we call a magic circle of play into existence, and the play goes on only while we keep the circle intact.

This means that any burden of reality imposed on a game will penetrate its magic circle and break the game. An online game is not merely slowed down, or encumbered, or altered by outside interference. It is annihilated. It is transformed from a game into ordinary reality. Thus the call to protect games is a request not merely to avoid burdening the world of virtual fantasy or to burden it less, but to leave it completely alone. We should think of online games as a nature preserve. They should be left *completely* untouched.

This only raises the further objection that fantasy is surely not that important. Why go to such lengths to protect fantasy worlds from outside actors?

Fantasy is the use of imagination and is integral to being human. Every scientific hypothesis begins in the imagination. Every policy proposal invokes a hypothetical world where things are better. Every virtual world is an effort to make our musings more concrete. Think of them as proposals for social worlds that people may want to inhabit. Virtual worlds represent concrete thinking about utopia. Utopian thinking may be problematic, and aimless fantasizing may be lazy; but imagining a new world and then *making it work for real people* offers a very important contribution to human experience. It is not just dreaming about change, it is dreaming about change and then trying it out. Virtual world builders combine the ideal and pragmatic. To encroach on their activity is to kill a goose that lays very fat golden eggs.

Even if we commit to the idea of protecting game- and fantasy-based virtual worlds as "virtual nature preserves," in practice we can't completely wall them off. It is hard to protect the magic circles we are now calling into existence. When a company makes a million-person game and fills it with virtual goods and networks of friendship, teamwork, and connection that persist over months and years, how can it prevent the blending of fantasy and real-world rules and behaviors? In the game, you are supposed to be The Hero and I am supposed to be The Sidekick. But in real life, you are The Twelve-Year-Old and I am The Dad. We can pull this off for a while, with you pretending to know everything and me pretending to be goofy and young, but we can't do it forever. Similarly, if a game allows the accumulation of tremendous economic assets, how natural would it be to sell those assets for real-world money? Any effort to keep virtual worlds a separate category under the law faces the practical difficulties of defining the kinds of behavior that are proper to those worlds.

Thus to treat games differently is not to exempt them from all oversight. On the contrary. For a game to escape the sales tax, for example, it may be necessary for it to meet carefully defined criteria for being a game. Just as religious organizations must meet certain standards to qualify for tax exemptions, games should have to meet certain standards for exemption from taxes and regulation. It is almost certain, for example, that to escape government intervention, games will have to be designed and managed so as to minimize the buying and selling of game goods for real money. This activity blurs the line between the real economy and the game economy, weakening the argument that the game world is special and different. What, after all, is the difference between the Diablo III Real Money Auction House and eBay? There isn't one. Thus it would be hard to argue that Diablo III's digital content should be exempt from sales tax. The authorities will have to develop standards to which a game must adhere in order to receive special treatment, and then monitor compliance.

While treating fantasy and business virtual worlds both fairly and differently will not be easy, it is certainly feasible and extremely important. Having such standards would allow the social hypothesis testing that we now see in online games to go on unhindered. The discoveries that will result are more than enough to justify the efforts we must make now to design the right policies: policies that protect online fantasy games almost as if they were an endangered species.

NOTES

INTRODUCTION

1. As I write, the total value of Bitcoins (a digital currency) in circulation is $1.5 billion, according to blockchain.info, a site that tracks the currency. According to the CIA World Factbook, this exceeds the total value of the money stock of thirty-three real countries (https://www.cia.gov/library/publications/the-world-factbook/rankorder/2215rank.html#top). Bitcoins are only a small part of the total virtual economy.

2. Brittany Darwell, "27M Users Bought Virtual Goods Using Facebook Payments in 2012; Zynga's Influence on Revenue Further Diminishes," Inside Facebook, February 1, 2013, http://www.insidefacebook.com/2013/02/01/27m-users-bought-virtual-goods-using-facebook-payments-in-2012-zyngas-influence-on-revenue-further-diminishes/.

3. European Central Bank, *Virtual Currency Schemes* (Frankfurt: European Central Bank, 2012), 15.

4. National Science Foundation Grant No. 1049449.

5. See Edward Castronova, *Exodus to the Virtual World: How Online Fun Is Changing Reality* (New York: Palgrave Macmillan, 2007).

6. BEA data from US Auto Sales, YCharts, http://ycharts.com/indicators/auto_sales, accessed January 28, 2013.

7. U.S. Department of Labor, U.S. Bureau of Labor Statistics, Consumer Expenditures in 2010: Lingering Effects of the Great Recession, August 2012, http://www.bls.gov/cex/csxann10.pdf.

I. WEIRDLY NORMAL

My research assistant on this project, Travis L. Ross, Ph.D., was absolutely indispensable. A great deal of what's written here originated in the work he did with our team of undergraduate "world explorers."

1. Data analysis software can write data to your screen and calculate things like averages. In many cases, this is immediately useful. Given a data stream about National Basketball Association players, a standard data software package can quickly determine the average height of players, a number that may be immediately useful in some context. With game economy data, however, the unrefined information you get consists of items like "the average price of (virtual) linen cloth on the Ashara Server from 1 A.M. to 4 A.M. on August 21 was twenty-three gold pieces." A statistician has lots of work to do in order to take numbers like this and put them together in ways that make the information valuable to a decision maker.

2. EVE Online is one exception: it has reported its economic statistics for many years.

3. See, however, E. Castronova, D. Williams, C. Shen, R. Ratan, L. Xiong, Y. Huang, B. Keegan, and N. Contractor, "As Real as Real? Macroeconomic Behavior in a Large-Scale Virtual World," *New Media and Society* 11 (2009): 685–707.

4. See "Worldwide Virtual Goods Market Reaches $15 Billion: Monetization Still a Four Letter Word," Superdata: Digital Goods Management, August 29, 2012, http://www.superdataresearch.com/monetization-is-a-four-letter-word/.

5. European Central Bank, *Virtual Currency Schemes* (Frankfurt: European Central Bank, 2012).

6. Being a nerd myself, I intend no pejorative.

7. Chances are you can still snag the card yourself: http://www.ebay
.com/itm/MTG-MAGIC-ISOLATED-CHAPEL-ALTERED
-PAINTED-ART-CARD-NIGHT-2-4-/280795424565?pt=LH_Default
Domain_0&hash=item4160b62735, accessed December 27, 2011.

8. If you are playing MtGO, you are working with a software program
designed and maintained by Wizards of the Coast, the company that makes
the game. That software program speaks directly and securely to the main
servers of the game. Within the software program are a series of commands
that allow you to trade with another player that you specify. Basically, you
propose a trade to Player X. Player X sees the trade terms and then has the
option of clicking Yes or No. If he clicks Yes, the server makes the trade
happen: it securely switches the ownership of the traded items within the
game's database.

9. See Cardhoarder, http://www.cardhoarder.com/store/index.php
?target=products&product_id=10925, accessed December 27, 2011.

10. See http://www.cardhoarder.com/store/index.php, accessed December 27, 2011.

11. Economic theory says that such situations cannot exist, at least not
for long. "Eventually," says the textbook, "an arbitrage trader will come in,
buying low and selling high, thus eliminating the difference." The key
word there is "eventually." In EVE, the amount of time represented by
"eventually" can be hours or even days, plenty of time for a real human
player to come in and make a profit. EVE's trade systems are built so that
only a player who has built up his character's trade skills can see these situations and respond rapidly to them. The trick for an EVE trader is to hunt
for buy-sell divergences, find them first, and move in quickly with lots of
cash and inventory.

12. See http://en.wikipedia.org/wiki/Icelandic_kr%C3%B3na, accessed
February 14, 2012.

13. Economist Nicholas Economides maintains a very useful website on network economics; see Economics of Networks, http://www.stern .nyu.edu/networks/site.html, accessed January 2, 2012.

14. See http://www.facebook.com/press/info.php?statistics, accessed January 3, 2012.

15. "Top Sites in Russia," Alexa: The Web Information Company, http://www.alexa.com/topsites/countries/RU, accessed January 3, 2012.

16. See http://developers.facebook.com/policy/credits/, accessed January 3, 2012.

17. Brittany Darwell, "27M Users Bought Virtual Goods Using Facebook Payments in 2012; Zynga's Influence on Revenue Further Diminishes," Inside Facebook, February 1, 2013, http://www.insidefacebook .com/2013/02/01/27m-users-bought-virtual-goods-using-facebook -payments-in-2012-zyngas-influence-on-revenue-further-diminishes/.

18. To find these data, see the following websites and select the time period of interest: http://www.federalreserve.gov/releases/h6, https:// www.cia.gov/library/publications/the-world-factbook/geos/us.html, http://www.federalreserve.gov/releases/z1/.

19. See "List of Countries by GDP (Nominal)," Wikipedia, http:// en.wikipedia.org/wiki/List_of_countries_by_GDP_%28nominal%29, accessed January 3, 2012.

20. Michelle King and Geoffrey A. Fowler, "Warner 'Likes' Facebook Rentals," *Wall Street Journal*, March 9, 2011.

21. Jeff Jensen, "Miramax Creates Facebook App so You Can Rent, Buy Movies. Will You 'Like' This?" Entertainment Weekly, August 22, 2011, http://insidemovies.ew.com/2011/08/22/miramax-creates-facebook-app -so-you-can-rent-buy-movies-will-you-like-this/, observed January 3, 2012.

22. Valve president Gabe Newell has claimed that someone made $500,000 selling items for Team Fortress 2; T. C. Sottek, "Exclusive Interview: Valve's Gabe Newell on Steam Box, Biometrics, and the Future

of Gaming," The Verge, January 8, 2013, http://www.theverge.com/2013/1/8/3852144/gabe-newell-interview-steam-box-future-of-gaming.

2. FORMS OF MONEY

1. Joseph Stromberg, "Scientists Use Snails to Trace Stone Age Trade Routes in Europe," Smithsonian.com, June 19, 2013, http://blogs.smithsonianmag.com/science/2013/06/scientists-use-snails-to-trace-stone-age-trade-routes-in-europe/.

2. "The Weirdest Currencies in the World," CNBC.com, http://www.cnbc.com/id/31763263/The_Weirdest_Currencies_In_the_World, accessed April 3, 2012.

3. Alan E. Kazdin, "The Token Economy: A Decade Later," *Journal of Applied Behavior Analysis* 15 (1982): 431–445.

4. I heard or read this observation early in my career, and now I cannot remember who said or wrote it. My thanks, whoever you are, and apologies for being unable to find your work despite much digging.

5. The roots of the word "haggle" are old Germanic words for cutting and striking. It is indeed costly to have to cut and recut every time.

6. From "Early Modern European Currencies," Emery Snyder.org, http://www.emerysnyder.org/projects/currency0.html, and "List of Currencies," Rutgers.edu, http://www2.scc.rutgers.edu/memdb/choosefromlist.php?db=spuf&type=from_curr, both accessed May 17, 2012.

7. I steal shamelessly from the much more famous *cuius regio, eius religio* ("Whose realm, his religion"), the formula adopted in 1555 to settle the first wars of the Protestant Reformation. In this application, I suppose it would be *cuius regio, eius pecunia.*

8. Charles Lane, "The Man Who Predicted the European Debt Crisis," *Washington Post*, December 12, 2010.

9. David Wolman, "Dream of Universal Currency Just Won't Die," Wired, December 27, 2011, http://www.wired.com/magazine/2011/12/st_essay_globalcurrency/. Readers interested in seeing more of the strange currencies afloat today should read Wolman's tour of contemporary currencies, *The End of Money: Counterfeiters, Preachers, Techies, Dreamers—and the Coming Cashless Society* (Boston: Da Capo, 2012).

10. Commercial paper is most similar to short-term securities sold by the government, such as Treasury bills. Here the line between security and money becomes fuzzy. Perhaps the one thing that makes commercial paper similar to other forms of money is the fact that it is not backed by any collateral. It is simply a promise to pay.

11. See http://www.cashyourmiles.com/faq.php, accessed February 12, 2013.

12. Eric Caoili, "Zynga, Amex Launch Prepaid Debit Card with In-Game Rewards," Gamasutra, May 22, 2012, http://gamasutra.com/view/news/170763/Zynga_Amex_launch_prepaid_debit_card_with_ingame_rewards.php; Jon Matonis, "Virtual Currency Exchange First Meta Closes $466,000 Funding Round," *Forbes*, April 10, 2012.

13. The *International Journal of Community Currency Research*, at http://ijccr.net/.

14. I thank Richard A. Bartle for providing much of the information in this section in personal conversation and in his book *Designing Virtual Worlds* (Indianapolis: New Riders, 2003).

15. Joshua Fairfield, "Anti Social Contracts: The Contractual Governance of Virtual Worlds," *McGill Law Journal* 53 (2008).

16. Edward Castronova and Joshua Fairfield, "Dragon Kill Points: A Summary Whitepaper," January 24, 2007, available at Social Science Research Network, http://ssrn.com/abstract=958945 or http://dx.doi.org/10.2139/ssrn.958945.

3. IS IT LEGAL?

1. Seth Lipsky, "What Is a Dollar?" *National Affairs* 8 (2011), http://www.nationalaffairs.com/doclib/20110623_Lipsky.pdf.

2. WebCite, http://www.webcitation.org/6CygqRiVv.

3. David Wolman, "A Short History of American Money, from Fur to Fiat," The Atlantic.com, February 6, 2012, http://www.theatlantic.com/business/archive/2012/02/a-short-history-of-american-money-from-fur-to-fiat/252620/.

4. See 79 U.S. 457 at http://supreme.justia.com/cases/federal/us/79/457/case.html.

5. Michael F. Bryan, "The Trime," Federal Reserve Bank of Cleveland, January 15, 2004, http://www.clevelandfed.org/research/commentary/2004/0115.pdf.

6. European Central Bank, *Virtual Currency Schemes* (Frankfurt: European Central Bank, 2012), 9–11.

7. Nonetheless, there are limits on the state's ability to force us to accept its money. The response to a frequently asked question at the U.S. Treasury site says that private companies can limit the kinds of state money they accept. The law forces a *creditor* to accept dollars of any form in payment of a debt. It does not force someone selling a good to accept dollars. You cannot force a car dealer to accept $40,000 in pennies. On the other hand, state laws that make bus lines accept pennies have passed judicial scrutiny; http://www.treasury.gov/resource-center/faqs/Currency/Pages/legal-tender.aspx, accessed February 11, 2013.

8. Bruce Champ, "Private Money in Our Past, Present, and Future," Federal Reserve Bank of Cleveland, January 1, 2007 http://www.clevelandfed.org/research/commentary/2007/010107.cfm.

9. Ibid.

10. Bryan, "The Trime."

11. "Defendant Convicted of Minting His Own Currency," Federal Bureau of Investigation, Charlotte Division, March 18, 2011, http://www.fbi.gov/charlotte/press-releases/2011/defendant-convicted-of-minting-his-own-currency.

12. Paul Caron, "The Tax Treatment of Frequent Flyer Miles: An Update," TaxProf Blog, July 7, 2008, http://taxprof.typepad.com/taxprof_blog/2008/07/the-tax-treatme.html.

13. IRS Announcement 2002–18, http://www.irs.gov/pub/irs-drop/a–02–18.pdf.

14. Gerry W. Beyer, "Citibank Claims Awards of Frequent Flyer Miles Are Taxable," Wills, Trusts, and Estates Prof Blog, March 9, 2012, http://lawprofessors.typepad.com/trusts_estates_prof/2012/03/citibank-claims-awards-of-frequent-flyer-miles-are-taxable.html.

15. Jamie Golombek, "Tax Expert: Traveller Wins Right to Claim Aeroplan Points," Canada.com, July 3, 2010, http://www.canada.com/health/Expert+Traveller+wins+right+claim+Aeroplan+points/3228774/story.html.

16. F. Gregory Lastowka and Dan Hunter, "The Laws of the Virtual Worlds," *California Law Review* 92, no. 1 (2004).

17. Joshua Fairfield, "Virtual Property," *Boston University Law Review* 85 (2005), available at http://papers.ssrn.com/sol3/papers.cfm?abstract_id=807966.

18. F. Gregory Lastowka, *Virtual Justice: The New Laws of Online Worlds* (New Haven: Yale University Press, 2010).

19. See http://www.ca9.uscourts.gov/opinions/view_subpage.php?pk_id=0000011049, accessed June 4, 2012.

20. Leandra Lederman, "'Stranger than Fiction': Taxing Virtual Worlds," *New York University Law Review* 82 (2007), available at http://papers.ssrn.com/sol3/papers.cfm?abstract_id=969984; Bryan Camp, "The Play's the Thing: A Theory of Taxing Virtual Worlds," *Hastings Law*

Journal 59, no. 1 (2007), available at http://papers.ssrn.com/sol3/papers
.cfm?abstract_id=980693.

21. Eric Caoili, "Japanese Social Game Networks Take a Hit over
Regulation Concerns," Gamasutra, May 7, 2012, http://www.gamasutra
.com/view/news/169887/Japanese_social_game_networks_take_a_hit_
over_regulation_concerns.php.

22. F. Gregory Lastowka, "Criminal Games," Terra Nova, August
17, 2005, http://terranova.blogs.com/terra_nova/2005/08/criminal_games
.html.

23. Liz Benston, "Chips No Longer Good as Cash," *Las Vegas Sun,*
March 9, 2007, available at http://www.casinocitytimes.com/article/chips
-no-longer-good-as-cash-49187.

24. Rhode Island State Law, Chapter 11, http://www.rilin.state.ri.us/
statutes/title11/11-19/11-19-9.HTM, accessed June 4, 2012.

25. Lastowka, *Virtual Justice.*

26. Sheppard Mullin, "Making Sense of Virtual Dollars," Law of the
Level, November 22, 2011, http://www.lawofthelevel.com/2011/11/articles-1/
virtual-currency/making-sense-of-virtual-dollars/; see also this slide deck
prepared by the law firm Perkins Coie in 2010: http://www.slideshare.net/
jonmatonis/virtual-currency-law.

4. IS IT MONEY?

1. Bruce Champ and Scott Freeman, *Modeling Monetary Economies*
(Cambridge: Cambridge University Press, 2001).

2. The best introduction to coordination games remains Thomas
Schelling, *Strategy of Conflict* (Cambridge: Harvard University Press,
1960).

3. Central banks attempt to manage inflation, even setting target inflation rates. Nonetheless, the Federal Reserve does not make inflation what

it is. Rather, it tries to respond to the changes the economy throws up. My point is that if the Fed did nothing at all, inflation would still occur.

4. Scott Rigby and Richard Ryan, *Glued to Games: How Video Games Draw Us In and Hold Us Spellbound* (Santa Barbara, Calif.: Praeger, 2011).

5. Byron Reeves and Clifford Nass, *The Media Equation: How People Treat Computers, Television, and New Media Like Real People and Places* (Stanford, Calif.: Center for the Study of Language and Information, 2003).

PART II. IMPLICATIONS

1. Gregory Clark, *A Farewell to Alms: A Brief Economic History of the World* (Princeton: Princeton University Press, 2008).

5. WEALTH, POWER, AND HAPPINESS

1. Dozens of these papers are linked at Professor Williams's website, http://www.dmitriwilliams.com/research.html.

2. Anthropologists have begun to explore the signification effects of virtual money. See Bill Maurer, Taylor C. Nelms, and Lana Swartz, " 'When Perhaps the Real Problem Is Money Itself!': The Practical Materiality of Bitcoin," *Social Semiotics* (2013).

3. In addition to black marketers, such technologies would be of use (and are probably being pursued) by terrorist and criminal organizations.

4. For a survey, see Bruno Frey, *Happiness: A Revolution in Economics* (Cambridge: MIT Press, 2010).

5. We are not the only species that trades. Female chimps will trade intimacy for meat.

6. See U.S. Department of Commerce, U.S. Census Bureau, http://www.census.gov/hhes/www/income/data/historical/people/, accessed February 7, 2013.

7. That the normal economy could make people unhappy is not a new point. See Tibor Scitovsky, *The Joyless Economy: The Psychology of Human Satisfaction* (New York: Oxford University Press, 1992).

8. Annie Lang, "Motivated Cognition (LC4MP): The Influence of Appetitive and Aversive Activation on the Processing of Video Games." Paper presented at the annual meeting of the International Communication Association, Sheraton New York, May 25, 2009, available at AllAcademic .com, http://www.allacademic.com/meta/p13157_index.html.

6. CURRENCY AND CONFIDENCE

1. Stephen Knack and Philip Keefer, "Does Social Capital Have an Economic Payoff? A Cross-Country Investigation," *Quarterly Journal of Economics* (1997): 1251–1288.

2. Seashells have been used as luxury goods and money for a long time. Seashell necklaces have been found in Cro-Magnon burials hundreds of miles from any ocean.

3. Consumer Price Index data, United States Department of Labor, Bureau of Labor Statistics, http://data.bls.gov/cgi-bin/surveymost, accessed February 11, 2013.

4. E. Castronova, D. Williams, C. Shen, R. Ratan, L. Xiong, Y. Huang, B. Keegan, and N. Contractor, "As Real as Real? Macroeconomic Behavior in a Large-Scale Virtual World," *New Media and Society* 11 (2009): 685–707.

5. I am reminded of a recent advertisement about nutty superstitions in sports fandom: "It's only stupid if it doesn't work." Accepting dollars in trade becomes stupid if dollars don't "work"—that is, if you can't trade them away again.

6. Chip Morningstar and F. Randall Farmer, "The Lessons of Lucasfilm's Habitat," in *Cyberspace: First Steps*, ed. Michael Benedikt (Cambridge: MIT Press, 1991), available at http://www.fudco.com/chip/lessons.html.

7. Once upon a time, one could find on the internet an essay titled "Confessions of a UO Gold Farmer." It seems to have disappeared, but I recall the story directly.

8. I am surprised that no one has designed a banking or credit card interface like this. Instead, whenever we want to buy something, we have to reenter our payment information.

9. We find that most game designers see the institutions of the economy as a nuisance, things to be set up in a way that "works" and then ignored. It is seen as essential to have a player economy, but once one exists, it is generally not exploited further to create satisfying experiences.

10. I leave to the reader the exercise of identifying those parts of the government budget that might qualify even today as "free money."

7. HOW MONEY WILL EVOLVE

1. William Riker, "Implications from the Disequilibrium of Majority Rule for the Study of Institutions," *American Political Science Review* 74 (1980): 432–446; Sue E. Crawford and Elinor Ostrom, "A Grammar of Institutions," *American Political Science Review* 89 (1995): 582–600; Randall L. Calvert, "The Rational Choice Theory of Social Institutions: Cooperation, Coordination, and Communication," in *Modern Political Economy: Old Topics, New Directions*, ed. Jeffrey S. Banks and Eric A. Hanushek (Cambridge: Cambridge University Press, 1995), 216–268.

2. The controversial biologist Richard Dawkins, in *The Selfish Gene* (Oxford: Oxford University Press, 1976), argued that many thoughts are subject to evolutionary pressures. He gave thoughts that act this way a name, "meme," and hoped to thereby to help us see our thoughts as being similar to genes. It is not clear how successful that move has been. It cannot be denied that the things we say and do can cause a thought to propagate throughout society.

3. Peter J. Richerson and Robert Boyd, *Not by Genes Alone: How Culture Transformed Human Evolution* (Chicago: University of Chicago Press, 2005); David Easley and Jon Kleinberg, *Networks, Crowds, and Markets: Reasoning about a Highly Connected World* (New York: Cambridge University Press, 2010), chapter 7.

4. Susanne Lohmann, "The Dynamics of Informational Cascades: The Monday Demonstrations in Leipzig, East Germany, 1989-1991," *World Politics* 47, no. 1 (1994).

5. They don't have to match in the sense of being exactly the same. Indeed, "the same choice" is a matter of perspective. When we all "drive on the right," we are indeed choosing the right side of the road, from our own perspective. But from my perspective, *you* are choosing the left side of the road, not the right. And your choice of the left side of the road matches my choice of the right perfectly. You've chosen the side of the road that I am not using, I have chosen the side you are not using, and that is the best for both.

6. It is not hard to imagine circumstances in which the U.S. government had the same policies as it does today, and yet the dollar had no value as a currency. Suppose, for example, that people expected the government to collapse within a year, and with it the ability to enforce the acceptance of dollars as legal tender. Or suppose that people expected new counterfeiting technologies to flood the market with undetectable fake dollars. These expectations could make the dollar almost valueless without any change in government choices.

7. On the other hand, the state accepts only this money in payment. Perhaps, indirectly, the state is making its currency good by promising to accept it in payment of obligations. It is hard to determine what "backs" the fiat money of contemporary governments. But that is my point: if the relation of state currency to value is difficult to discern, it is not concrete in the way that heavy metal money's value is.

8. "40 Years of Driving on the Right Side in Sweden," The Volvo Owners Club, September 3, 1967, http://www.volvoclub.org.uk/history/driving_on_right.shtml.

8. WILDCAT CURRENCY AND THE STATE

1. Viktor Mayer-Schönberger, *Delete: The Virtue of Forgetting in the Digital Age* (Princeton: Princeton University Press, 2011).

2. Clare Chambers-Jones, *Virtual Economies and Financial Crime: Money Laundering in Cyberspace* (Cheltenham, U.K.: Elgar, 2012); Jeffrey Sparshott, "Web Money Gets Laundering Rule," *Wall Street Journal*, March 21, 2013, http://online.wsj.com/article/SB100014241278873243732045783746113511252002.html.

3. Geoffrey A. Fowler and Juying Qin, "QQ: China's New Coin of the Realm? Officials Try to Crack Down as Fake Online Currency Is Traded for Real Money," *Wall Street Journal*, March 30, 2007, http://online.wsj.com/public/article/SB117519670114653518-FR_svDHxRtxkvNm Gwwpouq_hl2g_20080329.html; Richard Heeks, "Understanding Gold Farming and Real-Money Trading as the Intersection of Real and Virtual Economies," *Journal of Virtual World Research* 2 (2009), http://journals.tdl.org/jvwr/index.php/jvwr/article/view/868.

4. Vili Lehdonvirta, "Converting the Virtual Economy into Development Potential," World Bank, 2011, http://www.infodev.org/en/Publication.1056.html.

5. Audit rates have been rising for the wealthy in the United States, but remain below 5 percent for the vast majority of taxpayers. "Filing Taxes? Beware Sharp Increase in Audit Rates," *Forbes*, April 6, 2012, http://www.forbes.com/sites/robertwood/2012/04/06/filing-taxes-beware-sharp-increase-in-audit-rates/, observed March 21, 2013.

6. Jack M. Balkin, "Virtual Liberty: Freedom to Design and Freedom to Play in Virtual Worlds," *Virginia Law Review* 90 (2004).

7. F. Gregory Lastowka and Dan Hunter, "The Laws of the Virtual Worlds," *California Law Review* 92 (2004); Joshua Fairfield, "Virtual Property," *Boston University Law Review* 85 (2005), available at http://papers.ssrn.com/sol3/papers.cfm?abstract_id=807966; Benjamin Duranske, *Virtual Law: Navigating the Legal Landscape of Virtual Worlds* (Chicago: American Bar Association, 2008); Marques Tracy, "Antitrust Law and Virtual Worlds," *Journal of Business, Entrepreneurship and the Law* 3 (2010).

8. In the 1970s and early 1980s, governments dabbled in policy testing but gave it up (see, e.g., Overview of the Final Report of the Seattle-Denver Income Maintenance Experiment, May 1983, http://aspe.hhs.gov/hsp/SIME-DIME83/index.htm). The tests were huge, unwieldy, expensive, and impossible to replicate. They were also unfair, taking place as they did in real environments with real people. Virtual worlds, by contrast, would allow policy testing in limited, controlled, and replicable social environments.

9. John A. List, "Why Economists Should Conduct Field Experiments and 14 Tips for Pulling One Off," *Journal of Economic Perspectives* 25, no. 3 (2011): 3–16.

EPILOGUE

1. Joshua Fairfield first pointed out this danger and makes the case far more forcefully than I possibly could. His article deserves deep study; Joshua Fairfield, "Anti Social Contracts: The Contractual Governance of Virtual Worlds," *McGill Law Journal* 53 (2008).

2. Based on the dollar value of the rewards on offer, the Amex Reward Points seem to be worth about 120 points to the dollar. If so, Joe has paid Adam about $8. See http://www.membershiprewards.com/catalog/search/?N=11700000&mrnavlink=topnav%3aShoppingGiftCards&ResetBreadcrumb=true, accessed February 14, 2013.

3. For fuzzy cases, the best policy would be to clarify that any social media system not expressly designed for fun should fall under the serious category. The law should then state explicitly what a fun system must do to qualify as a fun-oriented system. Among other things, fun systems should forbid the use of the system for real-world economic gain in the form of advertising and currency trading and the like. It should be walled off from the real world to the greatest reasonable extent. In an early article, "The Right to Play," *New York Law School Law Review* 49, no. 1 (2004): 185-210, I argued that the legal recognition of fantasy spaces, which I called "interration," has a precedent in the legal recognition of fictional persons—which we know as "incorporation."

4. Johann Huizenga, *Homo Ludens: A Study of the Play-Element in Culture* (1938; Boston: Beacon, 1971).

INDEX